WYNN PLACE SHOW

A Biased History of
The Rollicking Life & Extreme Times of
Wynn Handman
and
The American Place Theatre

WYNN PLACE SHOW

A Biased History of
The Rollicking Life & Extreme Times of
Wynn Handman
and
The American Place Theatre

Jeremy Gerard

Smith and Kraus Publishers   2013

ISBN: 9781575258652
Library of Congress Control Number: 2013955569

Typesetting and layout: Elizabeth E. Monteleone
Cover: Jared Fries/Jared Fries Design
Cover photo: Martha Holmes
Author photo: Jennifer Barnette

A Smith and Kraus book
177 Lyme Road, Hanover, NH 03755
editorial 603.643.6431 To Order 1.877.668.8680
www.smithandkraus.com

For Tony Howarth and Julius Novick, critical inspirations;

Claire Reeves, Emily Gerard and Nick Gerard,
eternal inspirations;

and Wynn and Bobbie Handman, inspirations still.

A National Treasure

WYNN HANDMAN, a national treasure, came from the school of Meisner but understood all the techniques: Stanislavski's Method (as if), Stella Adler's (intentions) and Uta Hagen's (previous circumstances).

His teaching was not dogmatic; he wasn't a zealot about any one method or The Method, as so many acting teachers are. Wynn was more like a contractor, assessing the damage before diagnosing the problem and only then prescribing a solution. He would rid you of any and all bad habits you had acquired before meeting him.

In me, he saw a punk from Jackson Heights, Queens, New York with a mouth big enough to fit all the voices that would come out of it. Wynn never told me to close my mouth; rather he encouraged me to keep it wide open and further explore my own voice.

Wynn is a lover of words and of human behavior. Any play he had not seen, he had read. His insight into the American theater was the envy of every dramaturg. whether it be a romantic comedy from Neil Simon, or the emotional slugfest of Edward Albee and Sam Shepard. He loved the creativity and experimentation that found its way to his theater through the actors, designers, directors, and playwrights who had heard something new and exciting was going on at The American Place. Wynn was in love with the art itself, not the trappings of it.

I remember testing out *Mambo Mouth* in his class. It was so different than what the other kids were doing. Everybody is working on scenes from *Macbeth*, *Curse of the Starving Class* or *The Odd Couple*, and I come in as my character Pepe, an illegal alien who is entrapped by a scheme the INS used to use back in the day. Wynn sat there laughing and carrying on like any other audience member, but when I was done he cut into it like a surgeon trying to save an organ without killing the patient. He sat there quietly for a moment and then began to make suggestions. He told several anecdotes about Eric Bogosian and Spalding Gray, totally making a meal of it for us all. Then he got in to the history of one-man shows, and the difference between my writing and what Gray or Bogosian did.

His love of the work was so infectious it made you want to go out and see everything, read everything and be in everything. I've always admired those who subscribe to the philosophy, "If we all do well, I do well." Not the "everyone needs to fail for me to succeed" ethos that pervades show biz. That never was Wynn Handman's way.

Here's to an American theater god.

—John Leguizamo

Poster for John Leguizamo's *Mambo Mouth* (1990).
(Photo courtesy The American Place Theatre.)

Zoditch

SLIP THE DVD INTO the player and instantly you are transported to another time and place; it hardly seems like an Off Broadway theater in New York during the Vietnam era. The setting is a provincial Russian publishing house, and the focus is on a young man with a too-neatly trimmed moustache and rimless spectacles. A small man of endless grandiose small talk, nervous tics and adenoidal vocalizing — a performance of such detail and specificity and commitment that even over the distance of decades and the fifth wall of a television screen, you feel instantly that you know this character and have been drawn into this foreign place.

And then it hits you that you are seeing a very young Dustin Hoffman — he was 28 years old when this portrayal was recorded — and that in this performance as Zoditch, in Wynn Handman's American Place Theatre production of Ronald Ribman's *The Journey of the Fifth Horse,* are the trademark qualities that would soon make Hoffman a Hollywood star, from *The Graduate* to *Midnight Cowboy* to *All the President's Men* to *Kramer Vs. Kramer* to *Tootsie* — especially *Tootsie!* As the critic Harold Clurman memorably described it, the performance was "hysterical without feeling, grotesque without bitterness, touching without tears, funny without laughing."

For most people who came of age in the Sixties, as I did, the associations of that era are rock music, protesting the war in Vietnam, marching for civil rights, and having as much sex while trying as many varieties of drugs as possible. If you were that anachronism, a theater freak — even just a nascent theater freak as I was — the Sixties were also the Golden Age of Off Broadway. My father, a high school English teacher and poet manqué, had taken me to see *An Evening's Frost* at the Theatre de Lys on Christopher Street in Greenwich Village before my bar mitzvah. And because my high school drama teacher was a playwright, those years later in the decade were spent not only performing in his latest Pirandello-meets-the-suburbs provocation, but visiting the theaters that were providing sustenance and sanctuary for the most compelling dramatic voices of a convention-averse, angry, frightened, impatient generation. There would be the new rock musical at the Public Theater (*Stomp* by a visiting theater commune called The Combine, from Austin, Texas, as well as *Hair*, of course), and the unabashedly confrontational, sexually explicit *Dionysus in '69* at the Performing Garage, not to mention plays by Jean-Claude van Itallie and Lanford Wilson, Megan Terry and Rochelle Owens, Sam Shepard and Robert Patrick at Ellen Stewart's Café La Mama Experimental Theatre Club or the Judson Poets' Theatre among others.

All of those theaters were below Fourteenth Street. Broadway was a distant, irrelevant galaxy, its own Golden Age undone by the advent of those selfsame forces of anger and ecstasy — war, protest, the sexual revolution, mistrust of authority, rock 'n' roll music — that were feeding the downtown theaters and their adventurous, indeed ravenous audiences.

There was one significant exception. One downtown-type theater improbably situated within Broadway's shadow. One theater producing not the latest flaccid sex farce from London or bell-bottomed musical, but unabashedly experimental, risky new work by some of America's greatest living writers. These were artists who may never have given much thought to working in the theater until prodded to do so by a fevered coalition of Manhattan literati, left-leaning religious and political agitators, and, especially, disaffected theater partisans, all of whom had come under the spell of an unlikely breaker of molds named Wynn Handman.

With a vision sketched in pencil on the pages of a yellow legal pad, Handman had proposed a new theater that would demand as much of the audience as it did of the artists who served it.

Dustin Hoffman and Susan Lipton in *Journey of the Fifth Horse* (1966). (Photo by Martha Holmes.)

If you wanted to join the adventure, you'd better be prepared to sign on for the entire journey. There would be no single ticket sales — indeed, no box office! Attendance was restricted to season subscribers only. You had to be willing to invest in more than merely an evening's entertainment. You also had to forego the reassurance of critics telling you whether or not a show was worth your money and time, because critics were not necessarily going to be invited — that would be a matter for the playwright to decide — and there would be no traditional opening nights. You would be chancing an arm, as the Irish say, on talent and vision, just like the folks downtown, except that in this case the venue was St. Clement's, a failing Episcopal church on West Forty-sixth Street.

13

But if you were willing to take that trip, there was a good chance you'd encounter along the way such visionaries as the poets Robert Lowell and William Alfred, fevered young playwrights Sam Shepard, Ed Bullins, and Maria Irene Fornes, along with pre-stardom actors like Frank Langella, Roscoe Lee Browne, Joel Grey, Richard Gere, Olympia Dukakis, Sam Waterston, Faye Dunaway, Marian Seldes, Morgan Freeman, Christopher Walken and Mary McDonnell, not to mention Dustin Hoffman — well, the list goes on and on.

I was sixteen years old when I made my first trip to 423 West Forty-sixth Street in the spring of 1968. Who could forget his first encounter with a show called *The Electronic Nigger and Others*? It was an evening of three one-act plays by Ed Bullins, an ex-Black Panther-turned-comer in the wave of young black playwrights who were redefining the theater, demanding stage time with their white contemporaries and generally *epatering* the *bourgeoisie*. I was the guest of a black neighbor in suburban White Plains, where I lived at the time, a well-connected studio musician who'd been hearing Bullins's name and wanted to see what all the noise was about.

It would be another decade before I actually met Wynn Handman. In 1978 I was an addicted theatergoer and fledgling drama critic, and already any number of my most memorable experiences in the audience had occurred at The American Place. By then, the company had moved three long blocks east to 111 West Forty-sixth Street, where it occupied a space shoehorned into a brand new high-rise office tower.

Directly across the street was New York's legendary School of the Performing Arts and, next to the school, a Mexican restaurant called Xochitl, famed equally for its chicken molé and its animated pink neon sign depicting an Aztec Indian harvesting corn, or perhaps praying to it. That vertical beacon was well-known to the sailors on leave in the city who swarmed to it like moths. The theater was just half a city block from the eastern boundary of the Broadway theater district, but its heart and soul were well below Fourteenth Street.

That March I was reviewing The American Place Theatre's production of *Seduced*, Sam Shepard's garrulous yet moving meditation on the subject of Howard Hughes that featured an unforgettable, wildly over-the-top performance by Rip Torn as "Henry Hackamore," padding about the stage in Kleenex-box shoes, railing against injustices real and mostly imagined and warily desperate for some human connection.

Around that time I met, in addition to Wynn, a number of the other great driving forces in the movement to decentralize the American theater, to shift the focus away from the commercial nexus of Broadway to theaters dedicated not to box office but to developing artists and audiences.

What these visionaries had in common, along with their unshakeable devotion to new voices clamoring to be heard, was their own relative quietude. They were not themselves clamorers. They were not artists and, for the most part, they were usually content to let, no *devoted* to letting their artists be their voices and, ultimately, their legacies. I'm referring to people like Woodie King Jr., tireless champion of contemporary African-American writing at his New Federal Theatre; Ellen Stewart and Joe Cino, indomitable forces behind La Mama Experimental Theatre Club and Caffe Cino; Theodore Mann, founder of Circle-in-the-Square; Douglas Turner Ward, founder of the Negro Ensemble Company; Crystal Field and George Bartenieff, founders of Theatre for the New City; Curt Dempster, whose Ensemble Studio Theatre on West Fifty-second Street was a safe haven where theater professionals could develop new work and their own untapped talent. And that's a very short shortlist.

History can be indifferent, even cruel to the non-clamorers. Some years ago I spent an afternoon with Ellen Stewart at La Mama's historic complex on East Fourth Street in the East Village. This was in the years before the Internet made the business of archiving materials as simple as it has become, and La Mama herself — veteran of four decades not only producing new American playwrights but exposing New Yorkers for the first time to many of the world's most important theater artists — was convinced that her legacy eventually would pass with her as the larger culture was consumed by mass entertainment and both artists and audiences looked beyond the legitimate theater for sustenance.

Many of those legends are now gone, most recently as of this writing, Ellen Stewart, in January, 2011; Ted Mann, in February, 2012 and Irving Blau, co-founder of the San Francisco Actor's Workshop and later, with his Actor's Workshop partner Jules Irving, co-director of the Repertory Theater of Lincoln Center, in May, 2013; and, in June, 2013, Bernard Sahlins, a co-founder of Chicago's legendary comedy troupe, Second City.

Wynn Handman, teacher, director, nurturer and, most important, cultural pilgrim, has for more than half a century done meaningful, resonant work in the trenches of the American theater, much of it spectacular. You can see it in Hoffman's spellbinding portrait of a miserable, insignificant publishing-house factotum in *The Journey of the Fifth Horse* (still available on DVD) from The American Place Theatre's second season, in 1965-66. A daring performance by a young actor given license to take risks, it's just one high point among too many to count.

The source of such work must not go unrecognized.

WH leads a rehearsal of William Goyen's *Christy* (1964) at St. Clement's. (Photo by Martha Holmes.)

"Now the Théâtre-Libre must continue to fight its battle, so that its present generation of playwrights may not be forced to abandon the struggle and turn to newspaper or book as a means of earning their livelihood. It is absolutely essential that, when they write a good play, it shall be received and played in a house where they will be neither robbed nor strangled. The hostility toward the Théâtre-Libre has grown in proportion to its success."

from *Antoine and the Théâtre-Libre*
by Samuel Montefiore Waxman
Harvard University Press, 1926

WH in front of the United States Coast Guard Storis, outside
Narsassuak, Greenland ca. 1943. (Photo courtesy Wynn Handman.)

CHAPTER ONE:
BEGINNINGS

'A Place Of Serious Revelation'

THE CORNERS of the yellow legal pad papers are curled and brown with age and threaten to turn to dust in our fingers as we lift them from the dusty box to the big round table in Wynn Handman's office. But even after 45 years, the penciled scrawls still fairly bristle with energy.

NOTES ON
THE AMERICAN PLACE THEATRE
JULY-AUGUST, 1961   WH.

I make a mental note of the generous spacing between the first two lines, as if announcing to posterity the name of the enterprise that has been born with these nine simple, declarative words and one set of initials. No one has seen these papers since they were first set down and then stashed away in file boxes.

What follows on those faded, fragile leaves is a clarion call to arms:

"There is a plethora of entertainment," the handwritten notes begin. "While they are rolling down the hill, Americans are entertaining themselves to death. Movies, TV, Ball Games, stupid records, Bowling etc. and BROADWAY. They must stop and look, examine, learn, understand the truth of themselves. The Theatre can be a Place of serious revelation to Americans.

It is less and less this, it is not a serving, it is a calling. Nor are we, the serious artists in the theater, serving the purpose we were created for. If the serious plays are not written or done, we are leading meaningless lives; unless we do something now it will be too late. We will look back and say, 'we should have,' 'why didn't we?' and be bitter, dull and frustrated."

Wynn Handman reads aloud from the pages and a smile crosses his face as his own words transport him back to the summers of 1960 and 1961, when these thoughts consumed him. Although there were no troops leaning wearily into his every word, the notes have the force and passion of Henry V's St. Crispin's Day speech on the eve of the battle of Agincourt. In the competition for the American soul, they declare, the odds may be against us but our purpose is noble and we must at least put ourselves on the line trying.

For Handman, two decades had already passed since he'd found his calling, which happened in the most serendipitous manner.

"You have to go back to the fact that I was in World War II," Handman said. "I had my bachelor's degree from City College and I was a saxophonist in a jazz band. In December, 1942 I was inducted into Officer Candidate School." Bronx-born and raised in the Inwood section of Manhattan, a fingertip extending up into the southwest Bronx, Handman had returned to his home port of Boston after seeing action in the North Atlantic with the United States Coast Guard. One night he made his way to the Brattle Street Theatre in Cambridge, near Harvard, and saw Paul Robeson in *Othello,* a play it had taken the great African-American actor twelve years to bring from London, where his performance with a young Peggy Ashcroft had long since achieved the status of legend, yet which still was not deemed appropriate for Broadway's segregated theater.

"During the war I saw *Othello* with Robeson, and *The Skin of Our Teeth*, and a lot of Shakespeare," Handman recalled. When the war ended, he returned to New York.

"I was," Handman admitted, "equipped for nothing." On the recommendation of a friend, he made his way to The

Neighborhood Playhouse School of the Theatre on Forty-sixth Street between Fifth and Sixth avenues — the same block, as it happened, as the printing plant that Handman's father owned. Since 1935, the guiding spirit of the Playhouse had been Sanford Meisner, a brilliant acting teacher who had been a founding member of the Group Theatre and proponent of the Method acting technique devised by Konstantin Stanislavski and further developed in America by Lee Strasberg, Harold Clurman, and Cheryl Crawford. By 1946, the Group was gone, but The Neighborhood Playhouse, and soon the Actors Studio, replaced it as the bastions of Method training for serious actors and directors.

Handman was interviewed by Meisner himself and, notwithstanding his lack of experience, was accepted into the program. Improvisation was a hallmark of Meisner's teaching method, and Handman credits his gift for jazz improvisation for clinching the deal.

At table, WH (left) and Sanford Meisner with acting students at the Neighborhood Playhouse (undated). (Photo courtesy Neighborhood Playhouse.)

"I was home," Wynn said. "Meisner saw that I understood what he was getting at; I could communicate his meaning. His teaching method centered on finding truthful impulses in imaginary situations. He was strong on physical exercises and improvisation. I remember several were about abortion

— back then, that was not a typical subject for acting students anywhere else."

Meisner identified in Handman a quality that would change his life. Like the master, his student was a brilliant teacher. By his second year at The Neighborhood Playhouse, Handman was teaching the Meisner method.

In August, 1949, actor and politcal activist Paul Robeson joined the Handmans at Crystal Lake Lodge, in the Adirondack Mountains village of Chestertown, New York. WH headed a summer theater there with Neighborhood Playhouse students. (Photograph from the collection of Wynn Handman; fourth person unidentified.)

There was just one problem. In 1949, Meisner was pushing his star pupil to teach and direct; the star pupil, however, wanted to act. It was Handman's young wife, Barbara (known universally as Bobbie), who advised him to "Just do it," and follow Meisner's urging that he lead a summer theater at Crystal Lake Lodge in the Adirondack Mountains town of Chesterton, where a number of Neighborhood Playhouse students had formed a repertory company.

"I found myself, my calling, that summer. I have an aptitude for directing," he said, leaning forward in his oak and black leather-trimmed office chair, in front of the roll top secretary that has been the centerpiece of his offices since the founding of his theater. It's a ridiculously modest statement for someone whose nose for talent, unsurpassed teaching and

Jeremy Gerard

technical skills, and inextinguishable passion have had an impact on so many actors, writers, and directors.

Also coming into focus were Handman's stylistic, as well as aesthetic, differences with Meisner.

"Sandy was a brilliant, brilliant teacher, and I owe my career to him," Handman said. "But he could be mean, which is one thing I'm not." In 1955, Handman left The Neighborhood Playhouse and ventured out on his own as an acting teacher. He began to develop his own teaching style and technique. "Sandy developed these repetitive exercises," Handman observed. "They are so boring. All the Meisner teachers use them."

Actor Joel Grey had begun his studies with Meisner but continued with Handman.

"Wynn was gentlemanly, which was not always the case with Meisner," Grey recalled one morning in the spring of 2012, when he had settled into a long run on Broadway in a revival of Cole Porter's *Anything Goes*. "His openness and gentleness really gave people the confidence to do the work, which was quite naked and intense. He created an atmosphere of great trust and safety. He was never bitter or dark about the work. My God, he's so passionate about the theater! It was exciting to be a part of that."

Handman rented a studio in a carriage house on West 56th Street next to Patelson's Music House, across from Carnegie Hall. (He would spend the next 30 years teaching there before moving across the street into the Carnegie Hall Studios, where he taught until they were demolished in 2008. He continues to teach today in a studio on West Fifty-fourth Street, a few doors east of Studio 54.)

All the while, he was assimilating his experiences as a kid from upper Manhattan, as a veteran of the war, and as a student and teacher of an art that he knew was meant to serve a greater calling.

"Some people of my generation got infected with the idea that we have some purpose in life," Wynn Handman said. "We Jewish boys grew up with a need to make our lives meaningful. This was in me. And other things." Along with Shakespeare was the model of Bernard Shaw, whose classical music and drama criticism were as provocative and influential as his plays.

"I was affected by Shaw's criticism, and I wondered, *Where's the soul of the American theater?*" Handman mused, reading to me from one of Shaw's famous prefaces:

"The theater is as important as the Church was in the Middle Ages," Shaw had written. "When I wrote, I was aware of what an unofficial census of Sunday worshippers presently proved: that churchgoing in London has been largely replaced by play going. This would be a very good thing if the theater took itself seriously as a factory of thought, a prompter of conscience, an elucidator of conduct, an armory against despair and dullness, and a temple of the ascent of man."

"But the commercial theater," Wynn went on, "was the only theater we had, and too much of it was conspiring to make the American people soft-brained. It fed people the cultural equivalent of junk food."

And so Handman asked himself the question that would set his agenda: "What is most needed now? To tap the best talent. And get their plays on."

In the summers of 1960 and 1961, Wynn and Bobbie Handman vacationed on Fire Island with an ambitious young actor named Michael Tolan, who shared Wynn's sense of crisis about Broadway's vapid, obsessive commercialism, as well as his passion for new work. Together, they thrashed out an idea for a new theater. They agreed that while American literature and other arts had advanced intellectually, our theater had become paralyzed by Broadway's business model, in which only mainstream work had any hope of reaching a wide audience.

Handman in particular was impressed with what was unfolding in London, where George Devine and the English Stage Company were shaking things up at the Royal Court Theatre. Devine, who was producing the anti-establishment work of such artists as John Osborne and Arnold Wesker, was committed to establishing a theater company in which the writers were the stars.

24

"We have a choice: We must create a theater that will foster the serious, talented American writer to write plays for America today!" Handman scrawled on his yellow pad.

"NO SUCH THEATRE EXISTS," the pages all but scream out in capital letters. "SMALL ATTEMPTS EXIST (NEW DRAMATISTS, PLAYWRIGHTS' UNIT, CONTESTS, FOUNDATIONS, GRANTS TO OBSERVE AT HOUSTON, WASHINGTON, ETC.) THESE ARE VERY MINOR. THEY HELP A BIT BUT NOT ENOUGH TO VITALIZE AND MAKE A RECOGNIZABLE AND FORCEFUL INFLUENCE ON ANYTHING. THE URGENT NEED OF OUR TIMES CALLS FOR LARGE ACTION. WE MUST THINK AND ACT ON A BIGGER, HIGHER LEVEL THAN WE HAVE PERMITTED OURSELVES BEFORE — EVERYTHING UP TO NOW HAS BEEN PREPARATION FOR THE ACTION OF OUR TIME TO ESTABLISH THE AMERICAN PLACE THEATRE.

'The director's part is not well defined in this process, and mostly he should mind his own business and make the place for everything to happen. What is place? Place is anywhere that anything can happen!'
— Lawrence Kornfeld, Director

"I HAD NO THEATER, just an idea," Wynn Handman says. It is a Saturday afternoon in the summer of 2006, as the sun has begun its descent over the west side of Manhattan, pouring light into his office in the cramped American Place Theatre warren on the twenty-second floor of an office building on Eighth Avenue and West Thirty-seventh Street.

On a wall in the office is a quote from the iconoclastic American writer Gertrude Stein, part of which reads, "If anything is done and something is done, then *somebody* has to do it. Or somebody has to have done it."

The quote is among Handman's favorites, for two reasons. The first is that it perfectly captures the spirit of the founding of The American Place Theatre. The second is that it was written to honor the American photographer Alfred Stieglitz, whose An American Place gallery on Madison Avenue gave Handman's theater its name.

"I felt Gertrude Stein was admonishing *me*," Handman said. "*I* became the somebody."

In the early Sixties, neither the American mind nor the American theater were in quite the dire state that Handman's hand-scribbled notes suggested — at least not just yet. After all, the White House was occupied by a couple determined to restore glamor and cultural sophistication to Washington. A theatrical revolution of sorts had begun in London and was being felt in New York as newcomers — including Edward Albee (*The Zoo Story*) and Sam Shepard (*Cowboys*) and Jean-Claude Van Itallie (*America, Hurrah!*) and Rochelle Owens (*Futz!)* and Maria Irene Fornes (*Tango Palace*) were stretching the boundaries of conventional theater in Greenwich Village at places like Caffé Cino, a handkerchief-size space on Cornelia Street, and Café La Mama (later La Mama E.T.C., for Experimental Theatre Club) on East Fourth Street, and the Judson Poets' Theatre on Washington Square.

Uptown, Broadway producer David Merrick had set up a nonprofit foundation to underwrite the New York transfers of serious London hits like John Osborne's ferocious *Look Back in Anger* and boundary-breaking productions like Peter Brook's staging of Peter Weiss's *The Persecution and Assassination of Jean-Paul Marat as Performed by the Inmates of the Asylum at Charenton Under the Direction of the Marquis de Sade* (better known as *Marat/Sade*). On Manhattan's Upper West Side, Lincoln Center for the Performing Arts was taking shape, promising a new resident repertory theater modeled on the great European companies such as the Royal Shakespeare Company and the Comédie-Française.

But a paradigm shift was also taking place that would pull the theatrical spotlight away from New York City's commercial bazaar. In addition to the febrile Off Off Broadway movement, prominent directors were creating resident theaters around the country to foster talent outside Broadway, where careers (and fortunes) were all too easily made — or destroyed — overnight.

In Minneapolis, Sir Tyrone Guthrie launched his namesake theater in 1963 with a modern-dress *Hamlet* that quickly won international acclaim. In Providence, Adrian Hall founded the Trinity Square Repertory Company. In Washington D.C., Zelda Fichandler established the Arena Stage. In Houston, Nina Vance founded the Alley Theatre, and in Dallas the mother of them all,

Margo Jones — dubbed the "Texas Tornado" by *The New York Times* — was producing the premieres of plays by Tennessee Williams (*Summer and Smoke*) and Jerome Lawrence and Robert E. Lee (*Inherit the Wind*) and promoting theater-in-the-round at Theatre 47 (the name changed each January) at her intimate Art Deco building on the Texas State Fair grounds.

These theaters and their driven directors rejected the commercial model of Broadway. Indeed, they were being encouraged to do so by the Ford Foundation's cultural czar, W. McNeil Lowry. In 1962, Mac Lowry all but single-handedly launched the modern resident non-profit theater movement across America, funneling over $6 million in grants to professional local companies. Lowry was telling artistic directors to spend their money on art, not enterprise; anything less, he warned, and they would be cut off.

"Mac Lowry was interested in the arts," Handman recalled. "He was assigning fiction writers to theaters. He came to a reading we did of Bill Goyen's *Christy* and was tremendously impressed. He said to write a projected three-year budget for developing and producing new American plays. It must be subscription only, no box office."

Soon both the Ford and Rockefeller foundations were encouraging young writers to experiment and build resident companies of actors, directors and designers. They would be followed by the creation of the National Endowment for the Arts, which finally brought the federal government into the arena of cultural funding.

Broadway suffered from the brain drain. As Hollywood lured the best comedy writers to television and the golden age of musicals began its inexorable fade into irrelevance, New York's commercial theater establishment went begging. Theater artists, meanwhile, were learning that it actually was possible to earn a living — and even to do worthy work — beyond Broadway.

In the late Fifties and early 1960s, in addition to teaching his acting classes, Handman had been freelancing as a director Off Broadway. The most notable production he was involved with, in 1959, foreshadowed some of what would come later at The American Place.

"I directed a play called *The Power of Darkness*, a rare play by Tolstoy," Handman recalled. "Bobbie had prompted me to do a morality play, a peasant play. My *idée fixe* was to have Vladimir Sokoloff in it. I'd seen him in John Gielgud's production of *Crime and Punishment* — he was the Inspector to Gielgud's Raskolnikov. He'd studied with Stanislavski. He'd been a member of Max Reinhardt's company in Germany — he was Puck in *A Midsummer Night's Dream*.

Sokoloff agreed to do it.

The Power of Darkness opened Off Broadway on September 29, 1959, at the York Playhouse. In addition to a cast that boasted one of the English-speaking world's most respected actors, the show was notable for several other reasons. The Tolstoy adaptation had been written by Barbara Handman. The producer was Jan Murray, a Borscht Belt comic (and telegenic host of the wildly successful TV game show, *Treasure Hunt*) and student of Wynn's, and the company included several younger actors who would later show up on West Forty-sixth Street, notable among them Vincent Gardenia. The York Playhouse, at First Avenue and East Sixty-fourth Street, was owned by Warner LeRoy, who would transform the space a few years later into Maxwell's Plum, the quintessential Manhattan restaurant of the psychedelic, swinging Sixties.

Above all, however, *The Power of Darkness*, as its title promised, was not exactly your giddy-making, bubble-brained boulevard comedy. It wasn't even one of Chekhov's melancholy-drenched comedies. Emma Goldman called the 1886 play "a tragedy of sordid misery and dense ignorance." Despite some reservations about the performances of a mostly youthful American cast, *New York Times* drama critic Brooks Atkinson praised the play and Handman's production for being "brutally powerful on the stage."

"As a moral tale, it illustrates Tolstoy's sense of religious responsibility," Atkinson wrote. "But it is characteristic of Tolstoy in another respect. It illustrates his point of view about the peasant — a primitive, cunning, unscrupulous creature capable of shocking cruelty and deceit. It recalled the brutishness of a peasant revolt in *War and Peace*."

Stark Young, the dean of American drama critics, wrote to Handman, saying, "In very few cases have I carried from a production of one of the great plays such a feeling of general excellence, especially from Mr. Vladimir Sokoloff, one of the finest actors I have ever seen."

And no less a personage than United Nations General Secretary Dag Hammarskjöld responded, in a letter to Sokoloff, "My European heart rejoiced at the way in which in every detail you managed to let the inner light shine through in your interpretation."

Sidney Lanier (center) and WH receiving the Margo Jones Award from New York City Mayor John Lindsay. (Photo by Martha Holmes.)

That's not to suggest that Handman was averse to lighter fare (as he would later prove definitively with the introduction of the American Humorists series at The American Place). A diet of Tolstoy is bound to keep the coffers, not to mention the soul, yearning for change, and a few years later, fortune struck in the form of an ambitious young agent named Boaty

Boatwright and the beloved movie star Myrna Loy, both of whom would be drawn into the Handman circle.

Boatwright, now a veteran talent agent for International Creative Management (ICM), is a living nexus of several worlds in New York — creative types in film and theater, émigrés from the Southern states, Manhattan movers and shakers of every stripe, and progressive Democrats, all of whom would gather regularly for drinks and canapés in her gracious apartment in the Apthorp at Broadway and West Seventy-ninth Street. Myrna Loy, forever linked with William Powell as Nick and Nora Charles in the *Thin Man* films, was a Democratic party activist who, like Boatwright and Bobbie Handman, had worked on Adlai Stevenson's and later John F. Kennedy's presidential campaigns. At dinner with Loy one night, Boatwright, at the time a publicist for Universal working on Loy's latest film, *Midnight Lace*, put the idea of doing theater into her head. Having never before stepped foot onstage in a dramatic role, she was naturally reluctant, if no match for the determined Boatwright.

In her 1987 autobiography, *Being and Becoming*, Loy referred to the conspiracy to get her onstage as "the great swindle." The vehicle was to be a straw-hat circuit production of Leslie Stevens's paper-thin sex comedy, *The Marriage-Go-Round*, which had been a hit on Broadway for Claudette Colbert and Charles Boyer. Loy's co-star would be the more-than-respectable Claude Dauphin, and to prepare her for the demanding audiences of Ogunquit, Maine and Dennis, Massachusetts, not to mention Westport, Connecticut, would be Wynn Handman, serving as both director and private acting coach.

"There I was, framed by friends, with no visible means of escape," Loy wrote in *Being and Becoming*. "Wynn Handman began coming over to my apartment three or four days a week. We'd sit at the table by the window overlooking the city and he would talk about stage acting. We went through the script; then he broke it down and had me do the speeches. Subtly he introduced a very different medium, carefully nurturing me for this crucial step."

And so Loy made her stage début in Laconia, New Hampshire, in the summer of 1961. The production broke house records everywhere, Boatwright recalled. And, she added, as Loy quoted her in her memoir, "I never made so much money in my life. Wynn made a lot of money, Myrna and Claude made a lot of money . . . and we all had a wonderful time."

In addition to providing Handman with the financial wherewithal to start his theater, that tour of *Marriage-Go-Round* had other benefits as well.

"While coaching me for my stage debut, Wynn Handman shared his dreams of a place where American writers could experience theater, a creative environment where they could develop regardless of commerciality," Loy wrote. "Excited by the idea, I encouraged Wynn to proceed..."

That was only the beginning of Myrna Loy's connection to the Handmans, and to The American Place Theatre.

WH and Myrna Loy (undated). (Photo by Martha Holmes.)

CHAPTER THREE:
THE OLD GLORY

'What I was dreaming about was right there.'

AT THE ACTORS STUDIO, Handman had been invited into the exclusive playwrights' and directors' units. Under the direction of Elia Kazan, Lee Strasberg, Cheryl Crawford and Robert Lewis, the Studio was still the country's most highly-regarded training ground for actors, writers, and directors. It was also communications central, a place where the local currency was information, news, chatter, and gossip about what and who was hot on Broadway and in Hollywood.

"I wanted to direct," Handman said. "I became acutely concerned that if a play wasn't commercial — that is, for Broadway — there was no place for it." Of course, on Broadway, the serious dramas by established playwrights went first to Kazan, who had staged plays by Arthur Miller, William Inge and Tennessee Williams. If Kazan passed on a script, well then Broadway pretty much wasn't interested.

Handman, however, was looking for new writers for his theater. And not just playwrights.

"Robert Brustein was asking, 'Why aren't we getting Philip Roth and others writing for the theater?' " Handman recalled. "And George Devine wanted to know, 'Where is the mind in the American theater?' "

At the Actors Studio, Handman mixed with a crowd that shared both his ambition and his discontent. Kazan's wife, Molly Day Thatcher, was with the Writers' Unit, as was Nan

Lanier. Nan's husband, Sidney, was an Episcopal priest and second-in-command at St. Thomas's, a WASP bastion on Fifth Avenue. Sidney and Nan had met the Kazans in the Caribbean, when they were part of Laurance Rockefeller's crowd on St. John and Sidney ran a parish on St. Croix.

"I'd always had an interest in theater," recalled Sidney Lanier, a cousin of Tennessee Williams who was an irreverent reverend even before he gave up his cleric's robes altogether. "I was interested in communication; preaching is truth through personality, and that's what acting is, too. And remember, that high Episcopalian thing is very theatrical. It was acceptable transvestitism. I was reading existentialism, sitting near Sartre in a Left Bank café. In New York I was on a Sunday morning show on CBS called *Look Up and Live*, which we called *Look Up and Throw Up*. We had Albee and W.H. Auden on.

"Because of Gadge (Elia Kazan) and Molly, I became the first — and only — 'observer-participant' in the Actors Studio. Nan, my wife at the time, was Molly's assistant. Wynn was in the Directors' Unit, and it was through Nan that we met. Nan said he was talking about trying to start a theater.

"So I met with Wynn and Michael Tolan. With Wynn I would walk through the Theater District and see all the British names but a paucity of American voices."

For the first time, Handman was beginning to feel that time was running out. Or, perhaps, that the time, finally, was right.

"I had four years of the GI Bill, two years of which were at Neighborhood Playhouse," Handman said. "One year after, I had a year left. I wanted to marry Bobbie. She was from Elkins Park, an affluent suburb of Philadelphia. Her parents were hysterical." To calm their fears, he began studying for his master's degree at Teachers College. "I promised my future mother-in-law I was going to do speech therapy so she could tell the girls at the country club that I saw patients at the hospital three times a week.

"At Teacher's College, I read *America and Alfred Stieglitz*. I was influenced by Alfred Stieglitz's *An American Place*. I loved that book. Also Harold Clurman's *The Fervent Years*. Everyone was asking, *Where's the soul of the American theater?*"

In 1962 Lanier began planning with Handman. "I was at St. Thomas, where I was well-supported but trying to figure a way out of it," he said, "even though it was a good time to be there."

Lanier was aware of a failing outpost, St. Clement's Protestant Episcopal Church, on West Forty-sixth Street between Ninth and Tenth Avenues. He wanted to keep St. Clement's alive by having it play two roles, church by day, non-commercial theater by night. A key advantage to the plan, lost on no one, least of all Wynn Handman, was that The American Place would have a theater rent-free.

"I was pretty persuasive," Lanier said. "Bishop Donegan, the head of the diocese, wanted to be an actor but his mother wouldn't let him. I got St. Clement's, though I admit it was a little underhanded. But you have to remember, the Episcopal church ordained women priests.

"With Wynn, I was attracted to his enthusiasm, his warmth of personality. We enjoyed each other. We were both pastors, in a way. Wynn is a master of providing actors and writers with all the chicken soup they need. He cared about people. It wasn't about Wynn, it was about the theater."

Through another Actors Studio connection, Handman learned that Robert Lowell had written a dramatic trilogy called *The Old Glory* that the famed literary agent Audrey Wood was getting ready to send out to potential Broadway producers. *The Old Glory* adapted three tales — Nathaniel Hawthorne's *My Kinsman, Major Molineux* and *Endecott and the Red Cross*, and, centrally, Herman Melville's *Benito Cereno* — into an evening of verse drama. Wynn was determined to make it The American Place Theatre's debut production.

"Audrey Wood's assistant was Janet Roberts," Handman remembers. "She had *The Old Glory*. It was dripping with themes in American history. What I was dreaming about was right there! She said 'You're never going to get it, but read it.' Everyone turned it down. I was the lunatic who wanted to open with this play that ran four-and-a-half hours."

As it happened, Handman's partners were hoping to take things at a somewhat more modest pace. He already was working with writer and Actors Studio member William Goyen on his first play, *Christy*. Handman, however, would not be put off.

Frank Langella (standing) and Roscoe Lee Browne in *Benito Cereno,* the most successful section of the show that launched The American Place, Robert Lowell's trilogy, *The Old Glory.* (Photo by Martha Holmes.)

"He was totally going for broke," said Sidney Lanier. "He'd go for $50,000 when we only had fifty cents. He wanted to start with *The Old Glory*. I thought, *don't you think that's a little too ambitious?* But he was absolutely right. We wrote a manifesto, only about a page long, but we spent a lot of time on it. It was a very creative time. We felt we could make a difference. We felt we could tap people whose voices were not being heard. Robert Lowell said, 'Well yes, I think I could swim in these waters.' This became Wynn's passion. Wynn was the heart and soul of it.

"*The Old Glory* gave me a heart attack," Lanier continued. "It was just a huge undertaking. I wanted to start more humbly. Wynn stuck to his guns. I would wake up in the middle of the night worried about whether the furnace was working. But Wynn was right. It was his determination.

"I trusted Wynn's judgment, and I don't think I was ever wrong to do so."

Handman wasn't naive about what it would take to produce *The Old Glory*. It required a cast of fourteen principal players and twice that many extras. "The patron was Jean Bennett Webster," he said. Mrs. Webster was a prominent member of the St. Thomas congregation who later would marry Lanier. "She was a widow, quite affluent and interested in religion and theater," Handman recalled. "I started reading *The Old Glory* to her. She said, 'How much will it take?' I said $25,000. She said, 'All right, I'll do it.' I said, 'You are privileged to do this.' I was religious about it. I was messianic."

Yet another Actors Studio connection also signed on to Handman's dream early enough. Martha Holmes was one of a handful of women staff photographers at Life magazine beginning in the 1940s. Holmes had a special interest in artists; her portrait of Jackson Pollock at work is a classic that was the model for a U.S. postage stamp, and she was a regular presence at the Studio, photographing its iconic actors, directors and playwrights. Intrigued by the idea of The American Place, she began photographing it, as well, and would end up recording its entire history — not just the stars of its many productions, but the construction of its theaters, the changes in leadership, the public presence, right up until her death in the fall of 2006.

"We grew up in The American Place, my sister and I," recalled Terry Koshel, Holmes's daughter. "We would be there with my Mom as they were pulling out the pews and setting up the theater. All the writers knew us. They were like family. *We* were like family."

From the beginning, Holmes perfectly captured the frontier spirit of the American Place in her high-contrast black-and-white photographs of a very young Sam Shepard and Ron Ribman, of Handman conversing with Lowell or Lanier, of a radiant Faye Dunaway, an intense Roscoe Lee Browne.

On October 9, 1963, Sam Zolotow reported in his *New York Times* theater column that *The Old Glory* would be the first full production of the new, 165-seat American Place Theatre, located at St. Clement's Church. The director would be Dr. Jonathan Miller, who would be leaving his current job, appearing on Broadway in the hit revue from London, *Beyond the Fringe*, to make his directing debut with the Lowell trilogy. The show was expected to open early in the new year.

"*The Old Glory* couldn't have been a more appropriate play to open The American Place Theatre with," Handman recalled. "It was a huge thing to do, to open in a place that was not a theater. I wanted to open earlier in the spring, I was so eager. In 1962 there was virtually no non-profit theater. But we delayed 'til fall. We had to get the pews out, move the organ to the back of the church.

"In New York, Jonathan Miller fell in with the *New York Review/Paris Review* crowd," Wynn said. That included Lowell and his wife, *New York Review* co-founder and critic Elizabeth Hardwick. "Lowell didn't think of a Brit, he thought of a brain. He wanted Miller. He was on Lowell's wavelength. Miller had the vision."

On November 21, one month after the Zolotow item appeard, power socialites Ronald and Marietta Tree hosted a lavish Founders' Reception for The American Place Theatre at their spectacular townhouse on the Upper East Side of Manhattan. Among those assembled to hear board member Myrna Loy read Gertrude Stein's words about creating something called An American Place were Tennessee Williams, Robert Penn Warren, Lionel Abel, and America's poet laureate, Robert Lowell, who read from his work. Also among the guests were Suzanne Storrs. Suzanne would soon marry Lionel Pincus, the head of Warburg Pincus private investment bank. Suzanne would prove to be another of The American Place Theatre's most loyal and unwavering benefactors until her premature death at 60 in 1995.

The founders had not chosen an especially auspicious moment. Early the next morning, John F. Kennedy was assassinated in Dallas, bringing the age of Camelot to a violent, abrupt end. Other forces were also at work in the culture. The movement towards a theater serving American artists and local audiences was in fact taking root around the country. The Ford and Rockefeller foundations were actively taking on the role of American Medicis, in the absence of any organized federal policy of support for the arts, stepping in and nurturing the growth of the arts. And they had a lot of seed money to support that goal.

By the time *The Old Glory* opened nearly a year after that glittering reception, with a budget of $52,000 including running costs, The American Place Theatre had renovated St. Clement's, paid for with over $80,000 in contributions. The theater had been awarded a Ford Foundation grant of $225,000 earmarked exclusively for the development of new playwrights for the American theater. The Rockefeller Foundation had provided a second grant of $13,000 to finance workshop productions of new plays, including Goyen's *Christy*. And some $60,000 had been raised from 749 individual supporters, the *Times* reported, the most generous of whom were Jean Bennett Webster ($20,000) and Laurance Rockefeller ($7,000). Even the Shuberts, the embodiment of Broadway commercialism, contributed $1,000 through the non-profit Shubert Foundation.

A gathering of literary luminaries: Robert Penn Warren, Ralph Ellison, Elizabeth Hardwick, Robert Lowell, Sidney Lanier, WH, Donald Davis and, standing at left, Michael Tolan after *Brother to Dragons* (1965). (Photo by Martha Holmes.)

As the money fell into place, Miller and Handman began putting together the elements of the complex production.

"Wynn called me in to meet with Jonathan Miller," Frank Langella said. I was speaking to the actor in his London hotel in the fall of 2006, where he was ensconced for the duration of *Frost/Nixon*, one of the biggest hits of the West End theater season, in which he starred as the thirty-seventh president. "They sent me something to read, to prepare in advance."

Langella, who had been a student of Handman's, had just scored a hit Off Broadway in *The Immoralist* when, in the spring of 1963, he was invited to audition for a new play that would be the first production of a new theater.

"I remember standing at the lectern," Langella continued. "When it was over I remember Lowell looking at Miller with a look of excitement. Miller looked at Wynn and then Wynn said, 'We want you to do this.' I didn't have to go home and wait for the call."

Langella's co-stars would be Lester Rawlins and Roscoe Lee Browne. They would be performing in the centerpiece of the show, *Benito Cereno*, with Langella in the title role of a passive, broken-spirited captain of a slave ship.

"Roscoe and Lester Rawlins were the established old-timers. I was the new kid on the block," Langella recalled.

When told of Langella's recollection later that fall during a telephone call, Browne laughed. He had gone on to a distinguished career that combined classical acting assignments with stardom in Hollywood as both a film and television actor. But back in 1963, he was to play Babu, the mastermind of a rebellion on a slave ship. "I suppose I *was* a veteran," Browne admitted. "But we were really all novices, drawn together by the material as well as by Wynn's infectious enthusiasm and Dr. Miller's vision for this monumental work."

Miller's demands proved to be as ambitious as his vision.

"The company was friendly. My chief memory of the rehearsal process," Langella said, his tone betraying just a hint of lingering incredulity, "was that Jonathan began run-throughs on the second day of rehearsal." Which is to say,

·Miller expected the actors to have committed the entire threnody to memory practically from the start of rehearsals.

It quickly became clear to both Handman, as artistic director, and Lanier, as president of the company, that, however sure his overall vision of the work might have been, Miller was having difficulty with the nuts and bolts of an evening of operatic length whose three elements lacked a unifying theme or style. *Endecott and the Red Cross* was dropped from the program and consigned to a separate evening. Still, Handman was unhappy with what he was seeing on the stage. He called the acting "inorganic."

"Miller was brilliant conceptually," he added, "but he didn't have a clue how to work with actors."

Lanier concurred. He had been an actor before becoming a minister and was fully conversant with the practical aspects of putting on a show. "Jonathan Miller, well, the actors were totally mystified by his technique," he said. "Wynn and Michael would try to 'interpret' — I think he doesn't know to this day that they did that. He was very imperious."

Unbeknownst to Miller, Tolan and Handman began doing detail work with the actors at separate rehearsals, to guide them through the intricacies of the plays. "Wynn was a lovely presence with a streak of great kindness," Langella recalled.

Meanwhile, Lowell and Hardwick would sit in on rehearsals to watch the inventive young director. To them, theater was exotic — and perhaps hard to take completely seriously.

"Robert and Elizabeth would sit in the back, and he would take notes on a legal pad," Langella recalled. "Then he would fold it up into an airplane and fly it onto the stage."

The Old Glory wasn't the only thing going on at St. Clement's. Handman's work on the promising *Christy* was presented in a workshop (it never would move to a full production), as were pieces based on the writing of James Agee, and new work by Niccolo Tucci and Mary Lee Settle. Among the writers who signed up to develop new work for The American Place were May Swenson, Philip Roth, James Leo Herlihy, and Robert Penn Warren.

After delays caused by the extensive renovations to St. Clement's, *The Old Glory* began performances on November 1, 1964. *Fiddler on the Roof* had opened a few weeks earlier on Broadway and settled into the Imperial Theater for its record-breaking eight-year run. Days later, Lyndon Baines Johnson would win a landslide victory over Arizona Senator Barry Goldwater in the presidential election. But on November 1, the *Times* announced that a "New Theatre for New Playwrights" had arrived.

"One answer to the perennial question of where the new playwrights are to come from," wrote John Keating, "is given, with simple logic, by a new, non-profit organization called The American Place Theatre, from among all the writers of proven talent — poets, novelists, historians — who have, for one reason or another, never dared or desired to write for the Broadway theater."

The Old Glory proved to have been perfectly chosen as the vehicle for announcing the arrival of a new theater — of a new idea of theater. It was a demanding three-and-a-half hours of sometimes overwrought, sometimes turgid drama on Big Themes.

"I had not completely realized what my play was about — at least *all* the things it was possibly about — until I saw it illuminated by the director, Jonathan Miller," Lowell enthused. "My play is about revolutionary violence in American history and American culture. Jonathan Miller has transformed it into revolutionary theater."

If the critics got the message — and, given the promotional buildup the press gave to the opening, this was not likely to be a production ignored by the critics, whether or not they were officially invited — they also were cautious in their praise of the play, generally dismissing *My Kinsman, Major Molineux* as a failure but embracing *Benito Cereno* for its shattering theme and strong performances. They also were unreserved in welcoming new American writers to the stage; that certainly seemed like a good idea.

Nevertheless, most of the reviews can be said to have been at best circumspect, written partially in a kind of critical code that acknowledged the triptych's lofty ambitions without ever actually saying that these ambitions translated into exciting theater, as if this were somehow an impure thought. There were some exceptions, notably the poet W. D. Snodgrass in the *New York Review of Books*. Beneath the headline "In Praise of Robert Lowell," the review started off with a slap at the daily critics, "We cannot ask the reviewers from the Manhattan dailies to know a great play from a bad one."

Snodgrass went on to assert that he had "never been in a more excited and hopeful audience. We may yet have a theater of our own."

That last comment, like Devine's about the "soul" of the American theater, was a deliberate provocation to the theater community, such as it was. On the one hand, what were the works of Eugene O'Neill, Arthur Miller, Lillian Hellman and Tennessee Williams — not to mention Kaufman and Hart, Dorothy Fields, the Gershwins, Jerome Kern, Harold Arlen, Cole Porter, Rodgers and Hammerstein, etc., etc. — if not "a theater of our own," and one with more than a little soul? A theater so widely imitated that when John Osborne's *Look Back in Anger* detonated like a bomb at the Royal Court in London, all an American critic could do was say, *Well, it does bear a certain crude resemblance to* A Streetcar Named Desire. *When was that? Oh, yes,* ten *years ago.* After all, who was Jimmy Porter, raging drunkenly against authority, but an echo of Stanley Kowalski summoning the Napoleonic Code in his impotent efforts to rule a degraded world beyond his control?

On the other hand, every attempt to create an American equivalent of a "national" theater devoted to producing new works, even while serving as a curator and preeminent showcase of old ones, had failed, and would continue to fail, doubly the victim of America's squeamish inability to formulate a national culture policy and the siren call of Broadway — with its state-of-the-art productions, glamorous audiences and promise of riches — with which no subsidized theater could compete.

Writing in *The Nation*, Harold Clurman, a founding member of the Group Theatre who worked both sides of the footlights as director, teacher and critic, also welcomed Lowell to the fold even, he wrote cautiously, as "I dispel from my mind the fact that very few modern poets, novelists, and philosophers writing in English have written viable plays." After dismissing *My Kinsman, Major Molineux*, Clurman closely examined *Benito Cereno* and found its brutally violent conclusion — the slaughter of the rebellious slaves including, in the final, shattering image, their leader, Babu — discomfitingly ambiguous. In the end, Clurman wondered whether Lowell was most like his title character, "sensitive, lofty, impotent."

Reviewing *The Old Glory* in a revival for the U.S. bicentennial in 1976, Clive Barnes in the *Times* finally took off the gloves. Lowell, he declared, "knows as little about the theater as a church mouse at a bacchanalia, and his writing is too often dead and deadly." He accused Lowell, despite his "sincerity," of being "a tiresome, and obvious, bore..."

"I don't think Lowell had a really intrinsic sense of the theater," Miller later admitted to the poet's biographer, Paul L. Mariani. "I don't think he had a great visual sense, either, of how things might look. He was tremendously open to suggestions, totally humble about that."

In 1964, however, none of this mattered very much to either a cultural establishment hungry for something — *anything* — that would shake up the moribund uptown theater scene, or to theatergoers looking for an alternative to Broadway sentimentality. For theater cognoscenti, *The Old Glory* was the prestige ticket of the season.

"It was an extraordinary success," recalled Langella. "*No one* expected it. *The Old Glory* quickly became the show to see." Which meant that The American Place Theatre was signing up new subscribers by the hundreds. In January, Jean Bennett Webster underwrote the transfer of *Benito Cereno* from St. Clement's to the Theatre de Lys, a famed Off Broadway playhouse on Christopher Street in Greenwich Village, where it had a disappointing two-and-a-half month run.

"The critics were hard to take seriously," Handman said. "There was such diversity of opinion. I was slightly ahead of the time, and Clive Barnes wrote that you can't expect critics to be ahead of our time."

Lowell himself referred to the experience, according to Mariani, as a "raving *succès d'estime,*" and it can't be overstated how stunning a debut *The Old Glory* provided for The American Place. It would go on to win five Obie awards, including one for the Best American Play of the season (though, significantly, not one for direction). In the spring of 1965, the Rockefeller Foundation came through with yet another grant, this one for $154,000 to cover The American Place Theater's artistic and operational running costs. It was another important vote of confidence. In short order Lowell himself would be responsible for bringing Handman that most unexpected of gifts, a genuine, crowd-pleasing, box-office hit penned by another poet untested in theatrical waters.

The culture elite and the theatergoing public paid attention in equal measure and were eager to see what Handman in his church would come up with next.

Subscriptions, already up to 1,300, were increasing daily. That Handman already was being pressured to open a box office for single-ticket sales and to balance the demanding *Old Glory* with lighter fare — both of which were sternly, if unnecessarily, warned against by Mac Lowry — merely underscored just how right he had been when he'd scribbled his vision of a writer's theater on that legal pad some four years earlier. None of the success of *The Old Glory* would divert him from his mission.

"The review that meant the most to me was poet W.D. Snodgrass's," Handman noted. "He said, 'We may yet have a theater of our own.' That meant a lot to me, even though it was elitist. Joe Papp was always Joe Papp. I admired what he did. I didn't crave popularity. I said, 'There's mind in serious theater.' I wouldn't have called *my* theater the Public Theater, even though the work I was producing was highly eclectic. Joe was never as elitist as I was."

CHAPTER FOUR:
CHICKEN BLOOD, CANNIBALS, AND FAYE DUNAWAY

*'I had my doubts about killing a chicken onstage
every night.'*

HOW TO FOLLOW *THE OLD GLORY?* Even before
The American Place opened its doors, producers and agents
had begun inundating the young company with more scripts
than Handman and Lanier could possibly read. The newest
member of the team was Julia Miles, who "just showed up
one day to volunteer," Handman remembered, and didn't
leave for more than two decades. Miles, who had just had
a baby, had studied with Strasberg and worked at a small
theater in Brooklyn. "She had an aptitude for efficiency,
and intelligence," Handman said. "She became the general
manager, then associate director. She was on my wavelength
with taste in plays."

Miles recalls that time as one of unlimited opportunity.
"I said I don't know how to type, because I didn't want to
be a secretary," she said. "Wynn was more in charge than
Sidney."

"I was reading, doing whatever I was asked to do. I cared
about new plays and theater, and Wynn and I got along very
well. Those were the days when you could raise money."

Among the works that had piqued Handman's interest
was a one-act play, *Day of the Games*, sent in by an agent,
Sam Gelfman, on behalf of its unknown author, Ronald
Ribman.

"I read *Day of the Games* and my Geiger counter went *boom boom boom*," Handman recalled. "I called him and asked him for a new play. He sent me *Harry, Noon and Night*. It was so rich. It wasn't experimental, but it was wildly absurd."

Harry, Noon and Night was set in 1955 in Munich where Harry, a loser who cannot compete with his more successful straight-arrow brother, ultimately suffers a nervous breakdown. Harry's roommate, Immanuel, hunchbacked and homosexual, prods and cajoles him to his final meltdown; the play owes more than a little to Edward Albee's *Zoo Story* in its juxtaposition of straight and gay sensibilities and its themes of alienation and powerlessness.

Ribman's play lacked the high-toned intellectual pedigree of *The Old Glory*. An unknown poet and Keats scholar with a doctorate in English from the University of Pittsburgh, living in rural Johnstown, Pennsylvania, he'd turned out *Harry, Noon and Night* quickly. He was dazzled by the creative ferment at St. Clement's.

"It was a very, very exciting place to be," he recalled, speaking from his home in North Central Texas, where he recently moved to be near his grandchildren and to finish a novel. "You were always running into Lowell, Phil Roth. Wynn had a group around him — Sidney, Jean Webster, Julia Miles. Wynn always knew what he was doing, but they gave him ballast.

"My first impression remains the same today," Ribman said. "Wynn was bold in his judgment, adventurous, brave. Damn the tastemakers. He was never overwhelmed by reputation. He looked at the work.

"*Harry, Noon and Night* came out of my experience in Germany," he added. "I don't plot the way many writers do. It's a real exploration. I loved the collaborative experience — I had no idea it was done differently anywhere else. I'm going from being an assistant professor at some dinky college to working with Robert Lowell, Phil Roth, being on a panel talking with Lowell about poetry. It was absolutely exciting."

As with the Lowell plays, Handman was able to attract a gifted field of young talent for this Off Broadway premiere of a work by a poet-turned-playwright no one had ever heard of. The director was George Morrison, another Actors Studio veteran and favorite of Handman's. Cast in the leading roles of Harry and Immanuel were Joel Grey and Dustin Hoffman.

Joel Grey (standing) and Dustin Hoffman in Ronald Ribman's *Harry, Noon and Night* (1965). (Photo by Martha Holmes.)

"Dustin walked in off the street and just knocked everyone out," said Ribman.

The first performance was on March 17, 1965 and the show ran only long enough to play for The American Place's 1,300 subscribers.

"It was a shocking play," recalled Joel Grey, who just a few months later would shock the Broadway audience as the Emcee in *Cabaret*. "Wynn knew I was struggling to get out of the night-club niche. He thought I was the real thing," Grey recalled. "I was a romantic leading man, the hero, the American in love with this crazy transvestite. Dustin was this effeminate German, a role that really was a precursor to Ratso Rizzo in *Midnight Cowboy.*"

Harry, Noon and Night was picked up by a commercial producer and moved to the Pocket Theatre, an Off Off Broadway house. None of the principals moved with the show. Robert Blake took over the role of Harry.

"Dustin just walked out before the move, and it was devastating," Ribman recalled. "Wynn was pissed off. We also lost Joel Grey and Morrison. It was upsetting. But Robert Blake was unbelievably great as Harry, *maniacal.*"

According to Ribman, no one in the company was prepared for the reception accorded by the critics to *Harry, Noon and Night.* The kinder ones merely condemned it as a betrayal of the promise of *The Old Glory.* Norman Nadel, the influential critic for Scripps Howard's *New York World Telegram and Sun* wrote that *Harry, Noon and Night* was "a thoroughly disgusting play which I recommend to no one."

Nonetheless several critics, including Howard Taubman in *The Times,* pointed out that whatever their specific misgivings concerning *Harry, Noon and Night*, Ribman, they agreed, was a talented writer destined to do better work.

Not surprisingly, the young playwright found the reviews crushing. "I was expecting grading, like in college," Ribman recalled. "Walter Kerr said I was a stain on the American theater. I totally gave up the idea that the reviews had anything to do with what was up there. I was almost destroyed when I saw what was being said about *Harry, Noon and Night. Womens Wear Daily* critic Martin Gottfried got it. I drove down to Florida and I don't think I lifted my head up till Savannah, Georgia. Brustein and Gottfried were the first major critics to get my work. The artist is *always* out there." Significantly, however, no one, least of all Handman, thought of *Harry, Noon and Night* as anything other than one more step in the fulfillment of The American Place Theatre's mission. "Wynn didn't care about the reviews," Ribman recalled. "He cared about getting the play up."

As if to underscore the point, Handman quickly made good on his commitment to Ribman by immediately producing his next play (and four more over the next decade). At the same time, word had gone out to writers and their agents that a new theater had opened that was offering first-class productions and a high level of intellectual cachet.

Robert Lowell, exhilarated by his experience with *The Old Glory*, convinced his good friend, the poet and Harvard professor of English literature William Alfred, come to the city to meet with Handman. Writer Paul Goodman had a play. So did the poet May Swenson and *All the King's Men* author Robert Penn Warren and humorist Bruce Jay Friedman. There were even a few actual playwrights, including three African-Americans new to the scene: Ron Milner, Phillip Hayes Dean and Ed Bullins. All of these writers would be produced at The American Place in the early seasons.

"I'm responsive to the needs of our times," Handman said.

He felt much the same when Lowell secretly passed along Alfred's play *Hogan's Goat*. It had taken him nine years to complete and the author still wasn't prepared to send it out into the world. But Handman connected with it and conspired with Lowell to get the reclusive professor down to West 46th Street under the ruse of some unrelated activity.

Lowell had to practically drag William Alfred to Handman's office at St. Clement's. "He threw him into a chair and said, 'Read it,'" Handman recalled, recounting an ages-old tradition of having the playwright read his own script aloud. *Hogan's Goat* was the poignant coming-of-age tale, written in blank verse and set in the late 19th-century Irish Brooklyn, of brass-knuckles back-room political rivalries, family disputes and divided loyalties. And it was a love story about a ward leader determined to take on a corrupt system, and his long-suffering wife.

"I read everything aloud to Bobbie," Handman said. "We were weeping."

Faye Dunaway was a member of the foundering Lincoln Center repertory company at the time. She was 24 years old. The casting director brought her in to read for *Hogan's Goat,* Handman recalled.

"I thought she was very good," he said. "The mayor of Brooklyn was an important character; I couldn't cast that role.

Tom Ahearne had played Officer Brannigan in *Guys and Dolls*. He said, 'I don't work Off Broadway.'" Finally persuaded of the importance of the production, Ahearne signed on and "he was fabulous." When Jackie Kennedy said it was the best acting she'd ever seen, Ahearne told Handman, he'd confessed, "You know what that's worth to me? *Eight* Oscars."

Hogan's Goat opened to members in October 1965. In the leading roles of an idealistic ward leader who wants to take on the corrupt mayor, and his wife, were Ralph Waite and Dunaway. Along with Ahearne, the cast included Barnard Hughes and Cliff Gorman. The critics were invited in November, and this time there was not a lot of equivocating on their part. In the *Herald Tribune*, Kerr declared *Hogan's Goat* an instant classic that "stands as plainly, as simply, as possessively on the stage as though it had been born there..." Nadel, in the *World Telegram and Sun,* got over his disgust with Ribman and said that Alfred had written "one of the richest and finest American dramas to reach a New York stage in years." Perhaps unsurprisingly, the harshest criticism came from critics who'd been so supportive of the earlier work and felt betrayed by the play's relatively conventional dramaturgy.

Ralph Waite and Faye Dunaway in William Alfred's
Hogan's Goat (1965). (Photo by Martha Holmes.)

"I found the play completely uninteresting," sniffed Michael Smith in the *Village Voice*. Other critics also complained that *Hogan's Goat* wasn't avant garde enough. Handman bristled at such criticism, pointing out that he was being held to a standard he'd never set for The American Place.

"I was *not* an experimentalist. *Alternative* was the key word," Handman said. "I wanted to do plays that were an alternative to what you could get on Broadway. I wanted new voices worth hearing. I was not thinking in terms of experimental. But the Sixties blew up."

The buzz created by the critics and the contented theatergoers leaving St. Clement's prompted Lanier and Handman to extend the run a month longer than planned. Broadway producers came calling, but Alfred demurred, not wishing to accede to the demand for stars (as though he didn't have them already). So, with an assist from an outside producer and $12,000 put up by The American Place board, *Hogan's Goat* moved to the East 74th Street Theatre, a commercial Off Broadway house, where it ran for two years and more than 600 performances, returning $60,000 to the company's coffers. "*Hogan's Goat* was traditional in every way," Handman says, making no apology. "I did it for the language."

Hogan's Goat not only launched Bill Alfred's second career as a playwright, it also brought Dunaway to the attention of producers and agents, seeding the path to her Hollywood stardom.

The American Place would mount two more full productions during that critical second season. One was Paul Goodman's *Jonah*, an updating of the Biblical tale that would be embraced by neither the partisans of experimentalism nor the self-appointed guardians of capital-L Literature.

Goodman was the quintessential Manhattan polymath —essayist, novelist, poet, social critic, activist, provocateur — for whom the brief Biblical tale of a reluctant prophet and a pliant citizenry (not to mention a helpful whale) offered an easy parallel to New York City. The director was Lawrence Kornfeld, a co-founder of the downtown Judson Poets' Theatre, where he had staged several of Gertrude Stein's plays.

There was movement by the avant-garde choreographer and dancer Remy Charlip, who also designed the scenery and costumes. Another key element was the music, composed by Meyer Kupferman.

The title character in *Jonah*, as played by Sorrell Booke (who would go on to a different kind of fame playing "Boss" Hogg on the TV series *The Dukes of Hazzard*) was a Borscht Belt kvetch. "A prophet they need, you should pardon the expression, like a pain in the arm," he complains, when God's emissary, played by the great Earle Hyman, orders him to bring his End Is Nigh message to the not-so-good people of Nineveh. Jonah's wife was a cartoon shrew. "After all these years, He's sending you back to the small towns?" she whines.

Jonah was rushed into a full production not because it was ready but because it was the *most* ready of the plays in The American Place pipeline — early evidence that the company was not immune to pressure to keep the work coming. The attention heaped on *The Old Glory*, quickly followed by the success of *Hogan's Goat,* had made The American Place the place to be. Subscriptions were doubling each season and by the end of the decade the theater would have established a renewal record among subscribers that was the envy of the nonprofit world. This despite the fact that for every *Hogan's Goat* that appealed to a wide range of theatergoers, there were two or more *Harry, Noon and Night*s to test the patience, not to mention the intestinal fortitude, of subscribers.

Many in the audience for *Jonah* undoubtedly retained fresh memories of *J.B.*, the poet Archibald MacLeish's contemporary treatment of another Old Testament prophet, Job, which had run nearly a year on Broadway and closed just seven years earlier. *J.B.* had gotten the full Broadway treatment; staged by Elia Kazan and designed by Boris Aronson, it won every major prize that season, including the Pulitzer Prize. In the *Times*, Brooks Atkinson called it "one of the memorable works of the century," and "theater on its highest level."

That was hardly the welcome given *Jonah.* In the *Times*, Stanley Kauffmann called the play a mixed bag. "To every one of its virtues, a reservation must symmetrically be attached. It has imagination, but its imagination fails when most needed — at the end. It strikes an engaging tone but strays from it. It perceives its theme but dramatizes it inadequately." Kauffmann gave high marks to the production, especially Charlip's "enchanting" designs and Roger Morgan's "extraordinarily fine" lighting scheme.

"It adds up to what may be called a non-wasted evening, rather than a satisfactory one," he concluded, damning the show with the faintest of praise.

The other reviews were even harsher. In the *Village Voice*, arbiter of all things Off Broadway and sponsor of the Obie Awards, chief drama critic Michael Smith trashed the play as "clumsy, unfocused, and out of control" adding that the writing "has an errant, thrown-together quality." Smith went on to complain that because it was a subsidized theater, The American Place had "no excuse for playing everything so safe."

Well, let's consider: Thus far, Handman and company had produced an epic trilogy in verse (*The Old Glory,* which had won five Obies, including best play*)*, a play about a homosexual's nervous breakdown (*Harry, Noon and Night)*, a lyrical period piece (*Hogan's Goat)* and now an allegorical play by one of the country's most outspoken social critics. Somehow, "safe" doesn't quite qualify as an accurate description of that lineup. Indeed, it was during the run of *Jonah* that The American Place was named winner of the Margo Jones Memorial Award in honor of its commitment to "encouraging new plays and playwrights in the tradition of and vision of Margo Jones."

The other major production of the second season was *The Journey of the Fifth Horse*, Ronald Ribman's adaptation of Ivan Turgenev's *Diary of a Superfluous Man,* about the encounter between a self-important functionary in a provincial publishing house and an old woman servant who brings him a manuscript left by her recently deceased master, a hard-luck, lovelorn loser. As the master's story unfolds, the reader resists what the audience comes to see as the obvious, unsettling parallels between the lives of two desperate nonentities in an indifferent world. Turgenev's hell was the inverse of Jean-Paul Sartre's — not other people, but the long-hidden secrets of the soul finally revealed.

Despite the reception accorded *Harry, Noon and Night* (perhaps even because of it), Ribman had won a $6,800 Rockefeller grant allowing him to work on the piece.

"I loved Turgenev, especially *Diary of a Superfluous Man*. My taste was wandering all over," Ribman said. "But The American Place was my home. I always offered my plays to Wynn. He was always honest. When he likes something, he tells you. He laughs. He talks.

"With *Journey*, I had auditions and Dustin showed up. He'd walked out on me, but he was great. It was a very difficult production. Rip Torn, Susan Anspach — the three of them had a difficult time. Dustin would walk out and come back and say, 'I've been talking to my psychiatrist. He says I'm paranoid, that people *do* love me.' As for Rip, Wynn had to fire him. He was replaced by Michael Tolan, who was great.

"Once a play is out of your hands, it's got its own life. *Journey* won its awards. It was successful. At the Obies, I dared to thank the Rockefeller Foundation. Oh, my God. The Rockefeller gave me money to live on! Most writers are hanging by their fingernails. I thought they were going to grab the Obie out of my hands."

While the main stage productions were going on, Handman was also juggling a series of other shows in various states of readiness, putting all that foundation money to productive use. Robert Penn Warren's *Brother to Dragons* examined the murder of a slave by Thomas Jefferson's nephew in Tennessee. Handman's friend, the writer John Sachs, introduced him to a young humor writer named Bruce Jay Friedman, who submitted *23 Pat O'Brien Movies*. May Swenson was workshopping *The Floor*. Both, along with Andrew Glaze's *Miss Pete*, were presented under the umbrella title *Doubles and Opposites*.

Behind the scenes, as more and more subscribers were signing up, some personal intrigue was unfolding as well.

Sidney Lanier and Jean Webster had fallen in love, their affair the worst-kept secret in the disparate worlds of the high church and the rather less-high Off Broadway theater. Lanier had divorced his wife, Nan, and in May, 1965, gave up his pulpit. Bishop Horace W. Donegan — the same man who had turned St. Clement's over to Lanier and Handman three years earlier — granted his request to renounce the Holy Orders of the church (doubtless with a sigh of relief). Not long after, Lanier and Webster were married.

"I was looking for something bigger than religion even then," Lanier admitted. "I wasn't comfortable just being a secular humanist. I was kind of a weird Episcopalian priest. I was on the edge at all times."

The third season at St. Clement's included *The Displaced Person*, Cecil Dawkins's adaptation of four short stories by Southern Gothic writer Flannery O'Connor, and Niccolo Tucci's *Posterity for Sale*.

Reviewing *The Displaced Person*, Harold Clurman took the time to revise and to more fully articulate his own assessment of The American Place's work thus far:

"Most of the productions at The American Place Theatre have been received coolly," he wrote in the *World Journal Tribune* in January, 1967. "The organization's one outstanding success, *Hogan's Goat*, was by no means superior to several of its failures. Indeed, I have come to esteem Robert Lowell's *Benito Cereno*, part of *The Old Glory* triptych, more highly than I did on first seeing it. This was partly due to the fact that I went to see it a second time, a practice emphatically to be recommended for any but the most trivial performances." *The Displaced Person*, Clurman continued, "received notices which in the main ranged from indifference to scorn. The play has obvious shortcomings. It does not, for example, progress with sufficient dramatic tension; the pace of its writing is too even. But it has real characters; its situations are meaningful not only in regard to its environment — the backwoods of Georgia — but to much that is happening everywhere. It is not conceived as a smash; it is written with insight and humor for the compassionate understanding of unhurried folk whose sense of entertainment goes beyond titillation or nervous shock...I was more interested in *The Displaced Person* than many shows I 'liked' better!"

It is not conceived as a smash. For all his unease with the critical establishment, Handman did have champions (though Clurman, who wrote for the left-wing weekly *The Nation*, to be sure, would never be counted among the critical "establishment"), critics who actually did understand what he was attempting. Critics like John Lahr, later to become the chief drama critic of the *Village Voice* and then the *New Yorker*, who flouted the popular compulsion to see all art as a horse race, there to win the largest purse, make the biggest splash, and instead attempted to put what was going on at St. Clement's into a larger cultural perspective.

The season had opened in October 1966 with *Who's Got His Own*, a blistering torrent of anger wrapped in a play, unleashed by a young African-American writer named Ron Milner. Milner had started out under the protective wing of Woodie King, Jr. in their hometown of Detroit, and both men had moved to New York in the early Sixties, Milner to write plays and King to produce and direct, as well as act in them.

"I arrived in New York from Detroit in 1964, in a play by the Reverend Malcolm Boyd, an Episcopal priest," King recalled. "One of the places that we were familiar with was St. Clements and Sidney Lanier. Wynn took me in hand, and I appeared in *Benito Cereno* as a slave. I brought with me four or five plays and writers — *Who's Got His Own*, by Ron Milner, Ed Bullins and Charles Russell. I did readings at The American Place and Wynn eventually did them in full productions.

"In 1964, '65, '66, I was in and out of The American Place as carpenter, did readings of plays. Wynn had me sit in on all the major discussions with everyone from Robert Lowell to Ralph Ellison to Robert Penn Warren, Jonathan Miller. It was an unbelievable entrée to the New York theater world. My sense of Wynn was that, in his earlier days he had been a jazz musician, and that made him very comfortable around black artists. With his politics, and being a major acting teacher, well, he had really delved into the human condition. Although

60

he didn't go as far as the radical left, he did not turn away from the radical left. I did a film on black theater in America that Wynn was an integral part of. Ed Bullins was Minister of Information for the Black Panthers, and he was comfortable in The American Place Theater."

Who's Got His Own (the title is a homage to the Billie Holiday standard, "God Bless the Child") was developed in a workshop with King directing. But when he brought the play to Handman for a full production, Milner asked that another Detroit expat, Lloyd Richards, at the time the most prominent black stage director in the country (he'd shepherded Lorraine Hansberry's *A Raisin in the Sun* to Broadway) take over.

This was nearly eight years before Milner's *What the Wine-Sellers Buy* would become the first African-American-authored play to be mounted by New York Shakespeare Festival founder and producer Joseph Papp during his brief, tumultuous reign over the Vivian Beaumont and Mitzi E. Newhouse theaters at Lincoln Center.

In fact, perhaps no work produced by Handman until *Who's Got His Own* — not even *The Old Glory* or *Harry, Noon, and Night* — so clearly set The American Place apart from both the city's mainstream theaters and from the downtown theaters as well. It also crystallized Handman's despair over the state of the city's drama criticism, in which the critics from the major papers and other periodicals were uniformly middle-class, white, and male.

Milner's play captured an urban, African-American family in crisis, and the picture wasn't pretty. By this time, The American Place was regularly being reviewed, despite Handman's aversion to being judged by the critics.

Not surprisingly, most of the critics mistook Milner's rough edge for a lack of "eloquence or persuasion" as one critic put it. Virtually alone, Lahr, writing in Manhattan East, noted caustically that mainstream critics like Walter Kerr, at the *Times* and Richard Watts, at the *Post*, "can wax rhapsodic over the language and the passion and the overwhelming power of *Hogan's Goat*, but they find themselves totally uninspired by similar qualities in *Who's Got His Own*."

King never stopped supporting Milner despite his disappointment in having to turn the play over to another director; he put it most perceptively when he wrote, "Milner received a first-class production of his play and a second-class audience to approve its worth."

When King's New Federal Theater celebrated its thirtieth anniversary in 2000, Wynn was the guest of honor.

"Wynn is a pioneer in the old sense of making new ground," King says. "He's a rugged individual who says, *I'm going to take a shot and make a road for everybody to walk down.*"

Handman, whose memory of virtually everything ever produced at his theater remains as clear as if it had been yesterday, insists that *Who's Got His Own* "was a high point, both for me and for The American Place. In fact, it was easily one of the best plays we ever did, certainly in those first, crucial seasons.

Actor and producer Woodie King Jr., a friend who shared WH's vision of a non-commercial theater, founded the New Federal Theatre. (Photo by Jeremy Gerard.)

"But the critics weren't with us," he continued. "They just didn't get it. When the play traveled around the country, and even just up to Harlem" — where it was performed a year later at the New Lafayette Theatre — "well *those* audiences and those critics got it."

In midtown, however, *Who's Got His Own* — a vanguard play, a cry of anger and outrage — violated the established critics' sense of propriety. "Possibly Mr. Milner works at too high a pitch too much of the time," Walter Kerr opined in the *Times*.

Too high a pitch doesn't really begin to describe what the adventurous but unsuspecting members of The American Place Theatre were in for.

When Handman's acting student Joyce Aaron appeared downtown in early 1966 at Judson Poets' Theatre in *Red Cross*, a new play by her boyfriend, Sam Shepard, Wynn went to see it and was impressed. It had been only two years since Shepard, a transplant from California to the East Village, had seen his first two one-act plays, *Cowboys* and *The Rock Garden*, produced at Theatre Genesis (like Judson, yet another company in yet another church, St. Mark's-in-the-Bowery, on Second Avenue and Tenth Street). Intrigued and always looking for new young talent, Handman asked to see Shepard's next play.

"Me and Joyce had gone down to Mexico and *really* got sick," Shepard told me one morning over a long breakfast at Pastis, a trendy, bustling bistro near the apartment in Greenwich Village he shared at the time with the actress Jessica Lange. "And we came back, and I just wanted to get this play on. It was my first two-act play. It's strange, because I don't think it's been done since."

Called *La Turista*, in fact it was a *three*-act play that Shepard sent to Handman, who was happy to have it, whatever the length. "I thought the writing was superb," he recalled. "Albee's *Zoo Story* was a milestone because it dealt with alienation — of an individual. But by the late Sixties, it was about alienation of young people in society. That's what Sam was about.

Frances Foster (seated) starrred in James DeJongh's
Do Lord Remember Me with, from left, Charles H. Paterson,
Lou Myers, Glynn Turman and Ebony Jo-Ann (1982).
(Photo by Martha Holmes.)

"*La Turista was* a baffling play," Handman continued. "It was three-acts. Sam said he didn't want critics. I said I wanted Sam Waterston in the lead role. He got the part." *La Turista* would become the controversial centerpiece of the third season at St. Clement's.

La Turista represented not merely Shepard's first foray uptown; it was his first trip north of Fourteenth Street. It was also a venture into a world that bore little relation to the semi-improvised, seat-of-the-pants operations he was used to working at in the Village, with their tiny audiences of fellow playwrights and fellow-travelers, who bought cheap tickets on the night of performance. In that world, Shepard was a god who had infused theater with a rock 'n' roll sensibility, making it sexy, and dangerous, and alive.

And no one knew that better than Shepard himself. In new plays like *Ages of the Moon*, which had its world premiere in Dublin in March, 2009, Shepard has been looking back at his early work with a skeptical, not to say jaundiced eye.

"I was a belligerent asshole back then," he said in New York, a day before leaving to direct Stephen Rea in the new piece. "Really. I mean I was really not a pleasant person to be around. I was rude and belligerent." None of that fazed Wynn. When I asked Shepard what his first impression of Handman was, he answered, "Well, his extraordinary kindness and generosity. Genuinely. I can't remember Wynn ever coming in and giving his two cents' worth, like Joe Papp would, threaten to take over the show.

"Everything Wynn said about *La Turista* was very positive," Shepard continued. "He was always focused on the writer, even though his basic experience was with actors. He was so *devoted* to the writer, because I think he saw the potential for actors to get hold of new material. So when I brought in the play, it was a three-act play when we went into rehearsal with it, it was Sam Waterston and Joyce and a great director, Jacques Levy, who has since passed. We struggled and struggled with it. It was so long-winded, it just went on and on and on. And at the last minute, at the end of rehearsals, I pulled the rug out from under Wynn.

Sam Waterston (on floor) with Larry Block and Joyce Aaron in *La Turista,* Sam Shepard's first full-length play. (Photo by Martha Holmes.)

I said, 'Listen, man, it's too long, let's make it a two-act play.' He didn't even blink an eye. He just said, 'Fine, whatever works.' I just dropped the last act and made adjustments in the second act. It worked much better. And it was a wonderful theater, that church."

Length was not the only problem The American Place faced with *La Turista*. Waterston and Aaron played an American couple who, in the first act, become ill while on vacation in Mexico, and in the second are at home in an American hotel. In both acts, they're visited by witch doctors who perform various wild rituals to cure them, including, in one bloody, noisy instance, fowl sacrifice.

"I had my doubts about killing a live chicken on stage every night," Handman admitted. "I told them it was illegal." The creative team came up with a way of faking the death of the chicken, but the audiences were not assuaged.

"We lost a lot of subscribers with *La Turista*," Handman admitted. One letter began, "Three weeks after seeing Mr. Shepard's so-called 'play' *La Turista*, I'm *still* furious." In addition to generating a substantial sheaf of letters from angry subscribers, the play had aroused concern at the recently-formed New York State Council on the Arts, which had begun providing public funding to theater groups like The American Place and was not happy to hear stories of unhappy subscribers.

"NYSCA says 'Your subscriptions are going down,' or they read reviews by critics who don't get it," Handman said. "Something's *wrong* with that." Shepard had been one of the few writers bold enough or self-confident enough to have taken Handman up on his offer to not invite critics, and at first none came. But Lowell and his wife, the *New York Review of Books* essayist Elizabeth Hardwick wanted to see the play and to meet Shepard. Afterward, Hardwick published an effusively positive review of *La Turista* that caught everyone at the theater off guard. As with Snodgrass's review of her husband's *The Old Glory*, Hardwick took pains to insult anyone who did not "get" the brilliant if baffling new work, in this case, The American Place audience:

"The night I saw *La Turista*, The American Place audience was, for the most part, utterly depressing, middle-aged, middle-class, and rather aggressively indifferent; a dead weight of alligators dozing and grunting before muddily sliding away."

Hardwick, Handman recalled, made sure the other critics, who had not been invited to weigh in on *La Turista*, saw her review: "They thought I was rubbing their noses in it."

Yet Shepard, too, found himself unnerved by the subscription audience.

"The downtown theaters — Theatre Genesis, Caffe Cino, Judson Poets' Theatre, La Mama — that audience was just people off the street," Shepard said. "So that was an eye opener, that suddenly you were held prisoner by this audience of people who were putting their dollar down, and most of them were geriatric. I thought it was very strange, it seemed intrinsically wrong for a writer. You weren't getting the experience of an audience just coming in raw. This thing of subscription audiences is very troubling. I understand why it's a necessity economically, but I just don't like it."

Playwright and actor Sam Shepard in 1967 … and today. (left, Photo by Martha Holmes. right, Photo by Jeremy Gerard.)

Shepard conceded that his perceptions might have been influenced by the very large chip on his shoulder.

"It's still kind of an odd play, a pretty weird play," he said. "I wouldn't write a play like that now. I was totally arrogant then. I didn't read anybody else's plays, I didn't go to anybody else's plays. I *hated* theater. Everything was in this angry situation, it was Vietnam and everything. I carried a big grudge, I guess — the John Osborne routine. We were all angry young men. But Wynn was very tolerant. *More* than tolerant."

Handman rightly saw Shepard as the logical next step after Edward Albee in the evolution of American playwriting.

Perhaps Handman's most valuable asset was his ability to gain the trust of a wide range of artists and directors with their own ambitions and agendas. There's no better example of this than Woodie King Jr. whose, collaborations with white producers such as Joe Papp and Wynn Handman had put him in the forefront of the movement to bring pulsing, topical drama that dealt with race to mainstream audiences.

"Woodie gave me nine plays by Ed Bullins, thinking that he would be the one to direct them," Handman recalled. "But Ed wanted Robert Macbeth." By 1967, Macbeth had already founded his own uptown company, the New Lafayette Theatre in Harlem, and he was the more experienced director.

"I met Woodie and we became fast friends," Bullins told me. "He was a very humble, proud, tenacious type of spirit. He had goals and objectives, to be a producer. I remember going with him to see *What the Wine-Sellers Buy.* He was reaching out to learn how to produce, which he did.

"He took me to Wynn. They were very cordial, got along well. We had a nice meeting," added Bullins, who since 1995 has been a Distinguished Artist in Residence at Northeastern University and recently founded the Roxbury Crossroads Theater.

Handman chose three one-act plays for Bullins's first bill, to be presented during The American Place's fourth season: *A Son Comes Home, Clara's Ole Man,* and *Electronic Nigger,* the last serving as the deliberately oblique yet provocative umbrella title for the show, as well as its centerpiece.

"The production was a great educational experience," Bullins said. "I had been brought to New York by Robert Macbeth, who was starting the New Lafayette Theater in Harlem. We were doing workshops. I felt indebted to him. We worked well together. I told Wynn how I felt and left it up to him. Wynn said. 'You can have the director of your choice.' I chose Bob. Woodie stepped aside."

The Electronic Nigger and Others opened in March 1968, shortly before the assassinations of the Rev. Martin Luther King Jr. and then Robert F. Kennedy.

"Mr. Bullins is a welcome addition to the ranks of New York playwrights, and I saw the performance during one of the special evenings the more than usually enlightened management offers critics, rather than having an actual first night," Clive Barnes wrote in the *Times*, recognizing another of Wynn's innovations. Barnes added, somewhat patronizingly, that the evening offered "many moments ... when I was aware of the authentic presence of a dramatist." The three one-act plays, each different in style and tone from the others but all acutely tuned to themes of identity, community, and assimilation, announced the arrival of an important new voice.

"*The Electronic Nigger* put me on the map, theatrically," Bullins said. "Yes, The American Place was a white, Western theater with a middle-class audience. But Wynn really reached out to black audiences, young audiences, students."

Encouraging reviews of *The Electronic Nigger* set the stage for a commercial transfer, this time downtown to the Martinique Theater (where the triple bill's title was changed to the duller *Ed Bullins' Plays*.)

"Bob Macbeth had Joe Papp up to see the plays, and he was taken by what he saw," Bullins recalled. "He invited me down to see Charles Gordone's *No Place to Be Somebody*, which was really remarkable. Things just sort of leaped off from there.

"Wynn was a gentleman. He had a class operation. It was always obvious he had a love for the theater and for the people in it. I respected and liked him." Though he ultimately found an artistic home at the Public, Bullins had, in fairly quick succession, two more major productions at The American Place. "I became quite spoiled," he said.

For Handman, bringing African-American artists to The American Place was no minority program.

"I know there is no other theater — besides an all black theater such as the Negro Ensemble Company, which produced wonderful plays — that has such a collection of African-American theater," Handman says. "It's all diverse. Diverse, rich, experimental, and the plays get past black people being in the streets and taking drugs.

"When I started the theater, I knew there was an urgent need to include black drama, and there wasn't much around in '62

69

or '63. I did a staged reading of a play by an African-American novelist, John O. Killens, that Lloyd Richards directed.

"*Benito Cereno* had about 20 black cast members playing the slaves on the slave ship, and I got to know a lot of them. One of them was Woodie, who'd gotten off the bus from Detroit and headed for St. Clements. He became an actor around the theater. His best friend from Detroit was Ron Milner. Woodie directed a workshop of *Who's Got His Own*, but then Ron wanted Lloyd to direct it, he was the most acclaimed black director because of *Raisin in the Sun.*

"We did *Who's Got His Own* in the round. The play is very angry, about an angry man. It was like an operating theater. There was great tension emanating from the stage, and in the racially mixed audience as well."

Perhaps inevitably, some of the black productions at The American Place were about great, if sometimes forgotten, African-American performers. Many were brought to Handman by Woodie King, including Lonnie Elder III's *Splendid Mummer*, which starred Charles S. Dutton as the 19th-century classical actor Ira Aldrich. Roscoe Orman played the polarizing film actor Lincoln Theodore Monroe Andrew Perry, better known as Stepin Fetchit.

"That was *Confessions of Stepin Fetchit*," Handman recalls. "Perry, the actor who originally created the role, made a fortune. He was resented by black people because the character was shuffling, shiftless, mumbling and lazy. Perry was actually impersonating a rebellious slave who didn't want to work, so he made himself stupid and lazy. He was outwitting the white man. Perry rode around Beverly Hills on Rodeo Drive in his Cadillac."

The fourth season also saw the mounting, at long last, of *Endecott and the Red Cross*, the third part of Lowell's *Old Glory* trilogy that had been cut from the original production; and Ribman's next work, *The Ceremony of Innocence* (which drew on his background in academe and concerned the English King Ethelred the Unready; it was set on the Isle of Wight in 1013). The season was launched, however, with something unusual for The American Place: a new play from a relatively experienced hand, Frank Gagliano, who had actually been produced Off

Broadway twice before — and by no less eminent a sponsoring team of playwright Edward Albee and his longtime producer Richard Barr — before landing on West Forty-sixth Street.

Father Uxbridge Wants to Marry was the time-tripping fantasy, part hallucination, part memory play, about Morden, an elevator operator, on his last ride before he is to be replaced by an Otis automatic. During the ride, the elevator gets stuck, prompting Morden's mental escape, where he encounters a priest with unrestrained sexual proclivities as well as the various, uniformly unhappy women in their lives (all of whom would be played by Olympia Dukakis, in one of several shows she would be associated with at The American Place).

Olympia Dukakis in Frank Gagliano's *Father Uxbridge Wants to Marry* (1967). (Photo by Martha Holmes.)

Gagliano belonged to a kind of sandwich movement not bound by the old conventions yet not quite ready to leap whole-hog into experimentalism; if anything, *Father*

Uxbridge was a bit too timid, though that wasn't how most audience members saw it, and certainly not how it was received by the critics. They found it static and were unmoved by its hero's existential crisis.

None of this seemed to surprise the playwright.

"Let's face it (I have), all things considered in our theatre, it's not likely any other management would have attempted a production," Gagliano wrote to Handman when it was all over. "*Uxbridge* is too literate and experimental (in an honest, non 'in' way) for any other management to have taken a chance with it." Gagliano went on to extol another of Handman's innovations, the after-play discussions in which the audience was invited to stay and speak directly with the playwright, actors, director and others involved in the production. That was a level of audience-theater interaction virtually unheard of before then. The discussions went a long way toward giving The American Place subscribers a sense of being part of the theater's mission, not to mention a venue not only to show support or vent their frustrations, but to gain further insight into the plays from the people who created them.

By the tumultuous fall of 1968, The American Place Theatre had become established as exactly the kind of enterprise Wynn Handman and Michael Tolan had fantasized about eight years earlier on Fire Island: an alternative to Broadway and a beacon in the wave of new theaters springing up around the country. The American Place took chances both with artists and with audiences. Its programs were unpredictable and it could not be accused of adhering to any one style of show or promoting any one ideological line. The idea of subscribers, imperfect but economically essential to the survival of the developmental theaters, was becoming the norm, as were such innovations as flexible opening nights and after-play discussion groups.

While the downtown theaters, especially the Shakespeare Festival and La Mama, were also generating their share of excitement, Handman could boast one remarkable achievement even by their standards: The American Place won major Obie awards in each of its first five seasons, four of them for Outstanding Play of the Year (*The Old Glory*, *Journey of the Fifth Horse*,

La Turista, and Ronald Tavel's *The Boy on the Straight-Back Chair*; a second award went to *Glory*'s *Endecott and the Red Cross*, for design). That is especially noteworthy in light of the frequently icy critical reception — even from the Obies' sponsor, the *Village Voice* — and the fact that Handman was playing to a more straitlaced crowd than were his downtown competitors. And yet by 1968, The American Place claimed 6,000 subscribers, triple the number at the end of its first season.

One of the chief benefits of the acclaim and the interest of the theater-going public was that major writers now had an alternative to Broadway that offered first-class productions in a protected environment. Never content to coast artistically, Handman was in fact tempted to push the envelope even further.

Morgan Freeman and Mary Alice in Elaine Jackson's *Cockfight* (1977). (Photo by Martha Holmes.)

73

Soon, however, the stakes would become considerably higher. In September 1968, real estate mogul Larry Fisher announced that the tower he was building on the west side of Sixth Avenue between Forty-sixth and Forty-seventh streets would incorporate a new, underground theater complex specifically designed to accommodate The American Place Theatre.

But that was several years off. At St. Clement's in November, the first production of the 1968 season was George Tabori's *The Cannibals*, and it proved to be every bit as disturbing as *Harry, Noon and Night* and *La Turista*. Set at Auschwitz, the play revealed in uncompromising detail what happened when an obese inmate in a barracks of starving prisoners keeled over one day and died.

Tabori, a Hungarian Jew whose father was murdered at Auschwitz, was, like Sam Shepard a provocateur; his last play before *The Cannibals* was a program of one-acts called *The Niggerlovers* that confronted the American schizophrenia over race. *The Cannibals* had attracted the attention of choreographer and director Jerome Robbins, who was to stage it in a rare foray into the world of non-musical drama after winning acclaim for creating such spectacular — and spectacularly successful — Broadway productions as *Fiddler on the Roof*, *West Side Story*, and *Gypsy*.

"I've had my share of thrills, but *The Cannibals* experience was probably the peak," Handman recalls. "*The Cannibals* was a turning point in George Tabori's life. It was 1968, at St. Clement's. The original director, Jerome Robbins, couldn't cast it. I didn't want to fire Jerome Robbins, but George and I hoped he wouldn't do it, and he finally quit. Martin Fried directed. It was all about eating and survival. It had a great mix of styles, dark humor, moving speeches, strong dramatic interludes."

The cast included Bill Macy, later a co-star of Norman Lear's *All in the Family* spinoff, *Maude*, and a regular in Robert Altman's films. The gofer during the production, and also an understudy, was Harvey Keitel.

In his review of *The Cannibals*, Barnes took care again to compliment the "enlightened" leadership of The American Place for doing away with traditional opening nights.

"Mr. Tabori spares us nothing," Barnes then wrote. "This is not a play for the squeamish. Its details are gruesome and disgusting, and all the more disgusting for the intensity with which they are revealed." Barnes went on to compare the play to a "Kafka dream-world of private horror" and to Julian Beck and Judith Malina's Living Theatre troupe downtown, which had caused a stir with its hyper-realistic staging of Kenneth Brown's explosive *The Brig*. In the end, Barnes found the play too melodramatic to work fully as art, but at least he made it clear that such issues were of secondary, or at least subsidiary, importance. He almost sounded like Harold Clurman.

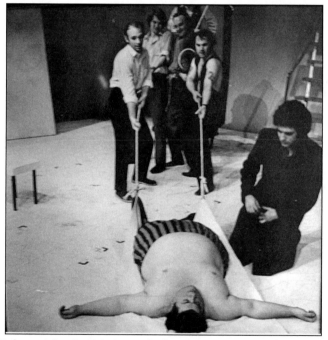

Before quitting the U.S. for good, playwright George Tabori pushed the envelope of taste with plays like *The Cannibals* (1968). (Photo by Martha Holmes.)

"*The Cannibals*, not for the first time, emphasizes the importance of this theater," Barnes concluded. "For here is a play, no masterpiece but worth producing, that Broadway and probably even Off Broadway couldn't touch. Yet The American Place can give it a staging that few of even our best American theatrical institutions could match."

"The New York critics were tepid," Handman recalled. Nevertheless, that was just the beginning of the unanticipated adventure he and Tabori would have when the famed Schiller Theater in what was then West Berlin invited the creative team to come over and stage the play for a German audience.

"I was treated as an honored guest, driven around in a chauffeured Mercedes," Handman says, not missing the irony. "In the cast were the offspring of Nazi soldiers. It was very tense. But on opening night there was a long silence, followed by huge applause, coming in wave after wave that kept building and refused to stop. George bowed and almost never came up."

Two and a half years later, Tabori would return to The American Place with *Pinkville*. This time the subject was Vietnam and in particular the massacre of civilians by American Marines at My Lai, along with allegations that the training of soldiers for combat in Vietnam was a kind of brainwashing that could only result in such atrocities. As with *The Cannibals*, Tabori gave voice to harrowing truths that could only make an audience deeply uncomfortable.

Pinkville was also staged by Martin Fried, and the creative team included modern-dance choreographer Anna Sokolow, a Neighborhood Playhouse alumna and protégé of Martha Graham's; electronic music by composer Jacob Druckman; and a cast that included two of Handman's more outstanding students from that time who would go on to fame and greatness: Raul Julia and, in the lead role of a young innocent who emerges a ruthless, psychotic murderer, Michael Douglas.

Pinkville would prove to be Tabori's American swan song. He soon returned permanently to Berlin, where he remained a major literary and theatrical figure for the next quarter-century.

76

"George had no future in this country," Handman said.

Tabori died in the summer of 2007; in its prominent obituary, The *New York Times* managed to cite not one of the plays that had put Tabori on the map in the U.S., nor was any mention made of the seminal role that Handman and The American Place had played in his career.

George Tabori's *Pinkville* starred Lane Smith and a young Michael Douglas (1971). Photo by Martha Holmes

CHAPTER FIVE:
BUILDING BOOM

'I was riding a big wave.'

IN THE MID-SIXTIES two inexorable forces — one commercial, the other cultural — threatened Broadway's existence. Real estate speculators were noticing that the theater district, roughly from Fortieth Street to Fifty-seventh Street, between Sixth Avenue and Eighth Avenue, was ripe for development. A building boom on the East Side of Manhattan was champing to move westward. Not even the most successful Broadway musical could turn the kind of profits generated by an office skyscraper. Besides, the area was rapidly sinking into squalor as a younger generation preferred spending its disposable income on rock concerts, record albums, and movies. There hadn't been a new theater built in the district in more than four decades. Forty-second Street itself, the "crossroads of the world," was overrun with tawdry porno theaters, massage parlors and other sex-industry operations. Going to a Broadway show posed unsavory challenges to tourists and suburban theatergoers, as muggers, panhandlers, and thugs competed with ticket holders for sidewalk space on the nearby streets. With thirty-odd historic theaters vulnerable to the wrecking ball and real estate interests eager to oblige, the city needed to act or risk losing one of its signature, if fast-fading, global attractions: the Broadway theater.

In October 1967, the City Planning Commission unveiled its response to the looming crisis. The area proscribed by those boundaries would be designated a Special Theater District.

Developers looking at the district were encouraged to include theaters in their building plans, in exchange for which they would receive zoning incentives allowing them to exceed established limits on square footage. In other words, put a theater in your skyscraper and you could add several more income-generating floors. Within two months, the city's Board of Estimate, with the enthusiastic support of the administration of Mayor John V. Lindsay, had approved the measure. Most of Broadway's theater landlords and producers were behind it as well. (The notable exception was Broadway's biggest landlord, the Shubert Organization, which controlled fully half the Broadway theaters and were skeptical of the city's commitment to enforcing the plan. The Shuberts were also precluded from benefiting from the plan because of a 1956 Justice Department consent decree making it nearly impossible for them to add any more theaters to their empire.)

Four theaters soon were in the works under the new plan. Two would be big, state-of-the-art musical comedy houses: one (the Minskoff Theatre) on the west side of Broadway between Forty-fourth and Forty-fifth streets, in a tower rising on the site of the legendary Hotel Astor; the other on Fiftieth Street between Seventh and Eighth avenues (originally called the Uris — now the Gershwin — it would be Broadway's biggest house, with more than 1,900 seats). The Uris site was also to include a 600-seat underground theater that eventually would become home to Theodore Mann's Circle-in-the-Square Theatre.

The fourth site, on the west side of Sixth Avenue between Forty-sixth and Forty-seventh streets, also would include an underground theater, not within the tower already under construction but as a separate, independent structure adjacent to the south, or Forty-sixth Street, side of the building.

In September 1968, Larry Fisher, speaking for Fisher Brothers, the developer of the site, announced that the new space — which would include a flexible, high-tech main stage seating approximately three-hundred people and a second, smaller space, as well as administrative offices and other amenities — would be leased to The American Place

Theatre for $5 a year for thirty years. The additional cost to Fisher Brothers for the structure would be around $2 million, although they would, of course, realize far more than that in the bonus commercial space the tower would get.

"It gives me a great feeling of satisfaction to do this for the nonprofit organization," Fisher told the *Times,* explaining that he had admired the work of The American Place.

A year later, at a ceremony honoring Lindsay's commitment to the project, the mayor lauded Handman and the new American Place, explaining that he had been determined to "make sure that in the expansion of the majesty of big office space on the West Side, we can stay ahead of the game in theater construction."

Handman knew he had been given a special mandate.

"The American Place Theatre was the first to be invited, because it was the most prestigious," he recalled. "Larry Fisher said I'd get the theater at Forty-sixth and Sixth. I personally liked the funkiness of St. Clement's. But the board wanted the new space. Mac Lowry set up to help us with the transition."

New York City Mayor John Lindsay at the opening of the
new space at 111 West 46th Street. (Photo by Martha Holmes.)

81

Whatever the attractions of St. Clement's funkiness, they paled before the thrill of creating your own space from the ground up (or, in the case of The American Place, down).

Unlike the funky space at St. Clement's, the new theater at 111 West 46th Street was sleekly modern. (Photo by Martha Holmes.)

"In designing the move, flexibility was in the air," said Handman. He and his established team of scenic designer Kert Lundell and lighting designer Roger Morgan worked closely with his hand-picked architect, Richard D. Kaplan, and designer Frank Trotta, creating a space capable of assuming multiple configurations, from standard proscenium-style to modified thrust. The walls would have movable wooden panels that allowed actors to enter from anywhere in the theater. Perhaps most significantly, a system of grids and catwalks suspended from the ceiling would allow unfettered access to the lighting system, a design that was revolutionary in its ease of use and flexibility, and which eventually would be copied in theaters all around the country.

In the meantime, however, Handman had no intention of letting anything get in the way of his theater's productivity while waiting for the new theater to be built.

"I was having a good time of it," he admitted. "I was riding a big wave."

The next three seasons saw The American Place building a kind of accidental company — of writers, as Shepard, Ribman, Tabori, Milner and Bullins all returned with new work — along with the design team and an expanding staff that included a dramaturg and script readers.

The 1969-70 season opened with *Mercy Street,* a first play by the Pulitzer Prize-winning poet Anne Sexton (a protégé of Snodgrass's) that was as psychologically raw, in its way, as Milner's *Who's Got His Own.* It featured Marian Seldes, another Neighborhood Playhouse alumna, as the adult poet, here named Daisy, recalling her thirteen-year-old self at the hands of an alcoholic, emotionally ruined and ruinous, sexually abusive, father.

"I loved Anne Sexton. She was so vulnerable and so in love with the theater," Seldes recalls, "and I thought *Mercy Street* would be so good for her, I thought a lot of churches would pick it up.

"I loved the play and I was very brave, you know. I said to the director, Chuck Maryan, `There's something missing in the play and the first act and the second act should be exchanged.' And he said, `You're absolutely right,' and we did it. If you're not afraid you'll be mocked, you can suggest something. But for me to suggest something to a writer? God almighty!"

While the Milner play had struck critics as artistically undigested in its depiction of a savage family dynamic, Sexton's play was attacked for its comparative modesty.

"Marian Seldes delivers these passages with a taut and abrasive clarity, skimming over nothing, making the naked words count," Walter Kerr wrote in the *Times,* going on to complain that among the play's "failures" was "its refusal or inability to name the sin or sickness at its center. We see the state that the girl is in now; we don't see the state that shaped it. In the end we become impatient. The victim has gone on too long without discovering enough."

Of course, the fact that children rarely are capable of articulating such private horror — that their inarticulateness may be the very element that gives a monologue its power — seems to have eluded Kerr. Inarguably, however, *Mercy Street* was *sui generis*, another American Place production that demanded to be taken on its own unconventional terms.

"I remember it was like heaven," Seldes told me, "because Wynn was so beautiful, in the first place, he was like a Greek god. I think I was a class ahead of him at the Neighborhood Playhouse. When I was there, I thought, well there are plenty of actors, what we need are producers who would say, 'Yes, I'm going to do this play.' That was Wynn. At The American Place he never pushed you and never seemed like someone coming in from the outside, and he was always *for* it. I think everyone felt that way. He was a very personal, hands-on person about his theater, and it *was* his theater, but you never felt it was an ego pushing him."

Sexton herself had only praise for her experience at the theater: "What's so beautiful about The American Place is that it's a place for *writers*," she told an interviewer. "They don't throw writers around and treat them mean. Wynn Handman, the director of the theater, and Charles Maryan, who staged the play, get you really involved and writing at your height. If you're not, they notice it and say, 'This isn't quite all you could do.' Then you write again, and it's better."

There were two more plays by African-American writers on The American Place agenda for the season, and they could not have been more different. Charlie L. Russell, brother of Boston Celtics basketball great Bill Russell, was the author of *Five on the Black Hand Side*, a zeitgeist situation comedy about an upwardly mobile family (the breadwinner is a successful barber) whose timid wife, having been radicalized by the women's movement, presents him with a list of demands to achieve equality in their relationship and family.

Had Russell's play charted a white family in similar circumstances, it probably would have been dismissed as innocuous, but this was new territory for black Americans —five years before television producer Norman Lear (an American Place Theatre supporter from the beginning) would spin off a sitcom from *All in the Family* to showcase Sherman Hemsley in *The Jeffersons*, about a black millionaire who, after making it in business, moves his family "on up" from the Queens of Archie Bunker to the toney Upper East Side of Manhattan.

84

Russell later adapted the play into a film, released by United Artists in 1973. While not a box-office hit, it was much-praised and established a cult following. It received a National Association for the Advancement of Colored People Image award for best screenplay. *Ebony* magazine recognized *Five on the Black Hand Side* as one of the ten best African-American films of all time.

Jerome Raphael and Marian Seldes in *Mercy Street*, a first play by the poet Anne Sexton (1969). (Photo by Martha Holmes.)

Then there was Bullins's *The Pig Pen*, also a zeitgeist play, but no sitcom. It was set in California on the night, five years earlier, of the assassination of Malcolm X in a Harlem ballroom. A mixed couple — he's black, she's white —is throwing a party for friends in an awkward if unspoken attempt to achieve racial parity. The evening is regularly disrupted by the sinister, furious intrusion of a billy-club-wielding white cop whose nickname gives the play its title. It was essentially plotless, all atmosphere, pregnant with portent. What it all meant was anyone's guess but one thing was clear: Bullins was coming of age right before our eyes, the most prolific and tuned-in of a generation of young African American playwrights. (Four years later, in 1974, Bullins's best — and most provocative — play, *The Taking of Miss Janie*, would open at Woodie King's theater, move to Papp's, and win both the Obie and the New York Drama Critics' Circle prizes for best play of the year. It was a drama that methodically dismantled every liberal cliché of black-white reconciliation currently in vogue, leaving nothing but the burn of acid in the mouth.)

"...there is a real feeling of time and place," Barnes wrote of *The Pig Pen*, which nonetheless mystified him. "It is like those parties you go to in what is laughingly called real life, and you hate the scene, go home, and suddenly find that it was a meaningful nothing experience. Mr. Bullins's play is the most meaningful nothing experience — and I intend this as a compliment — of the season."

A nothing experience, perhaps, for the clueless. Certainly most of The American Place subscribers *got* what was going on in *Pig Pen*.

"Our subscribers included a contingent of ladies from Hadassah," Handman recalled, "and they were *furious*. The black men were *screwing* this white Jewish girl! They were attacking me personally, and viciously, at the post-play discussions. Finally, one black subscriber stood up, identified himself as a former lieutenant of Malcolm X. and said, 'this play is about forbidden fruit.'"

Asserting its position as both discerner and arbiter of racial progress, as well as of what succeeded and what failed in the arts, the *Times* detected a trend and dispatched critic Martin Gottfried to weigh in on the matter. In a particularly obtuse Sunday essay headlined *Is All Black Theater Beautiful? No*. Gottfried condemned the Negro Ensemble Company as "rattl[ing] between a fear of being too militant for the moderates and too moderate for the militants," the result of which was the presentation of work at a "primitively parochial level..." By contrast, Gottfried wrote, Bullins had his plays done not at the NEC but at the very white American Place Theatre ("one of the most admirable theaters in the country"). Those were the "good" black plays produced by Wynn Handman, as opposed to the "bad" ones such as Charlie Russell's *Five on the Black Hand Side*, a play that was "embarrassingly naive, inviting benign and almost colonial approval from Handman's overwhelmingly white subscription audiences."

Gottfried argued that all art and artists must be judged by the same, color-blind standard and that anything else is bigoted. Nowhere in his essay was there any acknowledgement that those standards might be rooted in an ethnocentric worldview, or were given to change over time. Nor was there any evidence that Gottfried had ever visited the companies originating much of this work — the New Federal Theater and the New Lafayette. Applauding Bullins, and especially *The Pig Pen*, Gottfried attacked the critical establishment for overpraising Charles Gordone's *No Place to Be Somebody*, which Joe Papp had produced downtown and won the Pulitzer Prize: "Such overpraise, however well meant, is unintentionally bigoted, the result of white overcompensation and guilt," he wrote.

Artists must create art without racial consciousness and audiences must respond in kind, all of this taking place, one supposes, in some sort of neutralizing vacuum or in an eternal court before ancient Greek judges. (Of course, some of the best work that would soon be produced by the Negro Ensemble Company — especially plays by its homegrown stars Samm-Art Williams (*Home*), Charles Fuller (*A Soldier's Play*) and Leslie Lee (*Colored People's Time*) —were infused with just such "classical" qualities.)

Despite the salute to his theater, Handman was angered by Gottfried's attack on Russell and found it lacking in perspective. "Gottfried accused me of selling out," he said of the comment about *Five on the Black Hand Side*. "But Blacks hadn't gone through their *Abie's Irish Rose/Life With Father* period yet."

Handman's circle of supporters, going all the way back to the first days with the *New York Review of Books* crowd, always had a distinctly liberal, Upper West Side of Manhattan cast. By this time it had grown to include television writer and producer Norman Lear and his wife, Frances, who became close friends of the Handmans when they all were working on Eugene McCarthy's anti-war campaign for the presidency before the 1968 election.

"I first got to know them when Bobbie was working for Gene McCarthy," Norman Lear recalled. "I knew Sidney Pollack had studied with him. I'll tell you what I remember of Wynn. We were all in Nantucket at some grand place. And there was a piano. Wynn had a book of every song, and we must have spent three hours going through that book, singing around the piano. It was the rarest of events, as delicious as it could be. That for me is Wynn: He carries that light with him, it floods the room."

The final season at St. Clement's was also The American Place Theatre's most successful yet, a by-now typically eclectic mix of new work by writers untested on the stage, returning playwrights (Tabori with *Pinkville* and Shepard with a double bill), and new discoveries. The seventh season opened in November, 1970 with *Sunday Dinner*, a first play by the acclaimed and prolific fiction writer Joyce Carol Oates. It was a guilt-infused, symbolistic family play not unlike the longer dramas that were still years off for Shepard — *Curse of the Starving Class*, *Buried Child* and *A Lie of the Mind* — though, lacking Shepard's transmuting imagery and emotional underpinnings of sorrow and loss, it came across as dramaturgically clumsy and violently heavy-handed (or, as Harold Clurman, in a kinder mode, wrote in *The Nation*, "with an openness of declaration that is not altogether suited for the stage.")

The director was Curt Dempster, who shared Handman's commitment to theaters where artists were protected from commercial pressures; Dempster would go on to establish his own company, the Ensemble Studio Theatre, as a home dedicated exclusively to developing new work. The remarkable cast included Patrick McVey, Lois Smith, Jacqueline Brookes and Jerome Dempsey. As usual, even critics who hated the play applauded The American Place for a first-rate production; Clive Barnes commended the cast's "perky courage."

The company of Joyce Carol Oates's' *Sunday Dinner* (1970) included
Martin Shakar, Lois Smith, Brooks Morton, Patrick McVey,
Jerome Dempsey and Jacqueline Brookes. (Photo by Martha Holmes.)

Among the new works making their way through the development pipeline at The American Place was another first, a topical political revue by lyricist Ira Gasman and composer Cary Hoffman called *What's a Nice Country Like You Doing in a State Like This?* Not as edgy as *Beyond the Fringe*, yet edgy enough to fill a vacuum in a city that, during the years of the Nixon administration, was almost completely devoid of political humor, the studio production, as Handman called it, ultimately moved to a commercial Off Broadway theater, where it ran for more than five-hundred performances. The cast included future Broadway diva Betty Buckley in one of her first New York stage appearances. The show was also revived in 1984 at The American Place, the title slightly revised to *What's a Nice Country Like You* Still *Doing in a State Like This?* where it had another successful run.

An increasingly busy and in-demand Sam Shepard returned that season with the electrifying double bill of *Back Bog Beast Bait* and *Cowboy Mouth* — electrifying, that is, yet tricky business, mainly because the playwright's personal life was in such a shambles that producing them offered a serious challenge even for the normally unflappable Handman.

Cowboy Mouth, raucous, jangling, highly over-caffeinated, was Shepard's ecstatic collaboration with his girlfriend, the underground rocker and poet Patti Smith, problematic as he was married at the time to O-Lan Shepard, who'd just given birth to their son, Jesse. The result of all that tumult was a rehearsal period that was even more fraught than the one for *La Turista*. And then there was the run: several rocky previews — and exactly one performance.

"When we did *Cowboy Mouth* with Patti, I performed it one night and then split, took off. I thought *This is really too personal!*" Shepard recalled. "Any other producer would have had a shit fit."

Indeed, Shepard had just had a similar fiasco, on an even larger scale, with the Repertory Theatre of Lincoln Center, which had produced the world premiere of his tour-de-farce sc-fi melodrama *Operation Sidewinder*. How Handman remained sanguine in the face of such antics is almost beyond fathoming. And yet their relationship has been one of the most long-lived among the artists to have worked with Wynn, who would produce five more Shepard evenings of theater into the 1990s. In 2007, Shepard, still writing plays, agreed to serve as a trustee of The American Place.

"Sam writes in the subscribers' newsletter that he wants to be a rock star, not a playwright," Handman remembers with bemusement about the *Cowboy Mouth* experience. "It was absolutely wonderful, but then Sam wouldn't show up. You never know, when you do the creative act, what it's going to lead to."

Ronald Ribman's *Fingernails Blue as Flowers,* with Zakes Mokae
(from left), Albert Paulsen and Pamela Shaw (1971).
(Photo by Martha Holmes.)

'Moving to the big theater changed everything.'
Julia Miles, founder, the Women's Project

"THERE IS A 40-FOOT hole in the ground at 111 West 46th Street that may be the most important thing that has happened to American theater in a long time," wrote the *New York Times*'s influential architecture critic, Ada Louise Huxtable, in a remarkable appraisal of the new theater that appeared the morning after its official christening by Mayor John V. Lindsay on December 20, 1971. A double bill, comprising Ron Ribman's *Fingernails Blue as Flowers* and Steve Tesich's *Lake of the Woods* had begun performances at 111 West Forty-sixth Street a month earlier, on November 15th. The American Place was the first to open of the four new Theater District houses, and Huxtable praised the teamwork that had gone into creating an intimately connected series of adaptable spaces descending three stories below street level, the jewel of which was the 349-seat mainstage theater.

"The American Place Theater is fitted into a space behind the new J.P. Stevens building, put up by Fisher Brothers, at 46th Street and Avenue of the Americas as compactly and beautifully as a fine Swiss watch."

Reviewing the productions two days later, Barnes called the space "absolutely beautiful . . . handsome and gloriously viable . . . " before declaring both plays ambitious duds. Tesich (a prolific young playwright and Yugoslavian émigré who would go on to win an Academy Award in 1980 for his screenplay for *Breaking Away*) had already workshopped one play at The American Place, and he would have four more full-length plays produced there before his untimely death from a heart attack in 1993.

Even at this early stage of his career, Tesich was cultivating a neoconservative image, expressing disappointment in Americans who could not see how blessed we are and how responsible we must be for being a beacon to the world. *Lake of the Woods* was nebulous and somewhat inchoate, but it featured a memorable performance by Hal Holbrooke, just as Ribman's play, whatever its shortcomings, was galvanized by the performance of Albert Paulsen. It also introduced Zakes Mokae to American audiences; he would later anchor the plays of Athol Fugard in works such as *Sizwe Banzi Is Dead* and *Master Harold...and The Boys*.

Playwright Steve Tesich. (Photo by Martha Holmes.)

"Steve Tesich was my Right Wing," Handman recalled with a combination of sadness and amusement. "I got a play from an agent, *Division Street.* I thought *This guy is talented; the play won't work but we can develop something.*"

After *Lake of the Woods,* Handman would produce Tesich's *Baba Goya* with Olympia Dukakis, who'd become a member of the unincorporated American Place actors' unit. Ed Sherin directed. "It was 100 percent," Handman says.

I've come to understand that "100 percent" is highest praise from Handman, an accolade he reserves for directors he feels got the absolute best out of every element of a production, from the writing to the performances to the design team. Typically, a "100 percent" from Handman bears no relation whatsoever to a show's critical reception; indeed, the critics knocked Curt Dempster's staging of Joyce Carol Oates's *Sunday Dinner* as much as the play itself, yet it remains among the best-directed shows ever at The American Place, a "100 percent," without qualification, in Handman's estimation.

The second production of the inaugural season at 111 West Forty-sixth Street marked the return to the stage, after a four-year absence, of Jack Gelber. In the late Fifties, Gelber, working with Julian Beck and Judith Malina at the Living Theatre, had written *The Connection,* a landmark piece of realism about the lives of heroin addicts waiting for the next fix that was also made into a harrowing film. Gelber never wrote another play of comparable impact, but *The Connection* was enough to make his reputation. He went on to work as a novelist as well as playwright, and as a teacher with a legion of devoted students. His sole venture to Broadway, *The Cuban Thing,* opened — and closed — on September 24, 1968. *Sleep,* his first play since then, was a labored meditation on the personal failures of a middle-aged man meant to be a stand-in for all men or all Americans or some such, and it was met with a yawn from the critics. Nevertheless, Gelber was a dynamic presence and influence on The American Place community.

"*The Connection* became chic and brought success to Jack Gelber. That opened things up, gave people the courage to do things," Handman says. "Ed Bullins came in and told Jack he was responsible for him being a playwright. Bill Hauptman said *Action*, by Sam Shepard, got *him* writing. Eric Bogosian said Sam's *Killer's Head* got him writing monologues. You don't know how the work will have an influence."

By 1971 Sidney Lanier, whose active participation in The American Place had been diminishing for several years, was virtually out of the picture. His name no longer appeared next to Handman's above the title on playbills as President of The American Place; Handman had sole pride of place as Director, although soon Julia Miles would share the line as Associate Director.

(Lanier, whose affection for Handman and the theater they had founded never wavered, died early in the fall of 2013.)

The first season in the new theater was responsible for a series of discoveries, much as the first season at St. Clement's had been. Handman and Miles found Frank Chin, a thirty-year-old writer from the West Coast, and put Gelber in charge of staging his first play, *The Chickencoop Chinaman*. Stylistically, it was a little bit of Ron Milner and a lot of Sam Shepard — a hodgepodge of American mythologies and attitudes: the Lone Ranger appears, mask apparently hiding Asian eyes; there is a book called *Soul on Rice* about the New Asian taking power — and a simmering stew of anger aimed at everything from a sense of cultural malaise to the search for individual and group identity. The play made an instant star of an electrifying young actor, Randy Kim, who would make many more contributions as a member of The American Place's varied roster of exceptional talent.

As for Chin, he would return at the end of the following season with *Year of the Dragon* (also starring Kim), an even more sobering work than *The Chickencoop Chinaman*. To put Chin's work into context: *Chickencoop Chinaman* was the first mainstream production of an Asian-American play. It would be nearly a decade before David Henry Hwang, representing an even younger generation of Asian-American playwright, would have his first play, *F.O.B.*, presented by Joe Papp, and whose *M. Butterfly* would become, in 1988, the first play by an Asian-American to win the Tony Award for best play on Broadway.

Frank Chin's *Chickencoop Chinaman* (1972) starred Sab Shimono, from left, Randy Kim and Calvin Jung. (Photo by Martha Holmes)

Perhaps just as significantly, neither Chin nor Randy Kim was pigeonholed at The American Place. In their second season at 111 West Forty-sixth Street, Handman and Miles produced *The Karl Marx Play*, by Rochelle Owens. Owens was an internationally celebrated icon of the avant-garde theater; her play *Futz!*, an anarchic, antiestablishment tragifarce about a man and his erotic devotion to his pig, had been written in 1958, developed at the Guthrie Theatre in Minneapolis and premiered in 1967 at La Mama, which sent it on a European tour. *The Karl Marx Play* featured songs by *Hair*'s Galt McDermott and was staged by Mel Shapiro, a star from the Papp stable.

Casting it, however, was pure American Place.

"We held auditions for *The Karl Marx Play* and realized that Leonard Jackson, a black actor, had given the best audition for Karl Marx," Handman recalled. "Randy Kim gave the best audition for Engels. We didn't question it, that's just the way it was. We cast the best actors for the roles. We did non-traditional casting very early on." Like *Futz!*, *The Karl Marx Play* was sent on a European tour.

From *Karl Marx*, Kim segued right into Tesich's *Baba Goya*, a saccharine dream of excess whimsy about a Queens earth-mother and the eccentrics who busily circle her like gnats eluding slaps that never come. The *Times's* Walter Kerr loved *Baba Goya*. "Kerr always went with my right-wing stuff," Handman recalled.

WH and Julia Miles at the new theater at 111 West 46th Street.
(Photo by Martha Holmes.)

"Randy was in *Chickencoop Chinaman, Year of the Dragon* and *Baba Goya*. Exxon wanted to do *Year of the Dragon* on *Theater in America*, a rare Public Broadcasting Service series that brought theater to a national audience, but Randy turned it down," Handman said. "He hated the way he looked on TV. Randy Kim is *exceptionally* talented. The play did get on, with George Takei, who later became famous on *Star Trek*."

Takei said that, "Being in *Year of the Dragon* was probably one of the most thoroughly satisfying, fulfilling roles that I've had as an actor."

Kim would go on to co-found the American Players Theatre, in Spring Green, Wisconsin, an important resident company, where he has had the opportunity to play leading roles in the classics.

The Karl Marx Play provided another example of The American Place Theatre's early record of non-traditional, color-blind casting. (Photo by Martha Holmes.)

Handman and Miles were determined not to let the change of venue result in a change of character for The American Place, but from the beginning, that was a battle they were destined to lose. Even with rent set at a symbolic $5 a year, the move to the new theater inevitably changed the chemistry — and ultimately the DNA — of The American Place.

The larger space, the proximity to the Theater District, the attention that had been lavished on the new theaters and, certainly not least of all, the string of successes and the seemingly endless stream of literary figures and stage talent, actors, directors, and designers passing through, intensified the critical scrutiny Handman and company were under while ratcheting up the pressure to fill the seats. Moreover, rent or no rent, everything cost more in the new space. The staff was expanding with the list of subscribers, artists willing to work for little money at St. Clement's were less willing to do so in the new space.

And where once The American Place had been virtually alone among uptown companies offering new work to adventurous audiences, now there was competition springing up like wildflowers all over town. On the Upper East Side Jeff Jeffcoat, a young public relations consultant and sometime journalist, had been charmed by London's "chamber theaters," where small groups gathered for private readings of new plays. In 1970 Jeffcoat founded the Manhattan Theatre Club in his own living room, and soon the group would move to the Bohemian Benevolent Society on East Seventy-third Street, backed by such enthusiasts as Anne Jackson and her husband Eli Wallach, Stephen Sondheim, Ogden Nash, and Mildred Dunnock.

After eight years of disasters and defections, the Repertory Theatre of Lincoln Center gave up the ghost; in 1973 its two theaters, the Vivian Beaumont and the Forum (later renamed the Mitzi E. Newhouse) were turned over to Papp and became northern outposts of the New York Shakespeare Festival. Papp vowed that he would "bring the revolution uptown," and to some extent he made good on that promise, mounting such provocative new plays as Miguel Piñero's searing prison drama *Short Eyes* and Ron Milner's *What the Wine-Sellers Buy*, cheek by jowl with revivals of *Trelawny of the "Wells"* and *The Threepenny Opera* across the fountained plaza from the homes of the New York Philharmonic, the New York City Ballet, the New York City Opera and the Metropolitan Opera.

Other Off-Broadway companies that were beginning to make their names producing new work included Circle Repertory Company, home to the remarkable, long-lived partnership of playwright Lanford Wilson and director Marshall W. Mason; Playwrights Horizons, which produced comedies by Wendy Wasserstein and musicals by Stephen Sondheim and newcomer

William Finn; Curt Dempster's Ensemble Studio Theater; the Chelsea Theater Center, and the WPA Theater, along with revival specialists such as the Roundabout Theatre Company, which had started out in a subterranean space underneath a supermarket street in Chelsea before inching its way uptown.

All of these companies used subscriptions to build audiences, and while some of the artists affiliated with them had come out of the same Greenwich Village cauldron as Sam Shepard and Ron Tavel had before showing up at The American Place, the newer companies were in fact patterned more on the regional theater model, with their resident playwrights and companies and their generally more mainstream fare. As everything around him was in a state of creative upheaval and economic meltdown, Handman stayed the course while pushing to build the membership.

"The other theaters didn't change us," Julia Miles said. "Your taste is your taste."

Some of the best talent in the city was finding Handman, but not always at The American Place.

"After Harvard I enrolled at the Neighborhood Playhouse, but I got to New York and didn't want to be in school. I did believe the Meisner technique was the best in America," said André Bishop, a seminal producer in the post-Sixties nonprofit theater. "I got into a class with Fred Kareman, who taught with Wynn in a studio next to Patelson's," he continued, referring to the music store behind Carnegie Hall famed for the breadth of its sheet music selection for classical musicians. "This was in the mid-70s. You started with Fred and if you were good, you went on to study with Wynn. I got in and started working on scenes. Everyone said Wynn also worked with a lot of stars and models.

"What Wynn had for *André*, as opposed to someone else, was his passionate interest in text, which is not true with every acting teacher." Bishop said. He was brilliant at finding a play and giving it to you. He knew I was very good at language and gave me a great deal of Shaw and O'Casey. He knew Shaw was mind *and* heart, a fever pitch of emotion. Wynn would talk about jazz, verbal riffs. He did not give me

O'Neill or Williams. He was also brilliant at pairing you up with someone not necessarily the best for you but who had something you didn't. Wynn was not into gropey-feely, he was into delivering the goods. And he was great at getting new plays, by Donald Barthelme, Sam Shepard. I learned more about writing than acting."

Handman's best students usually found a way to cross over from the acting studio to The American Place, even if it meant working as waiters in the mid-theater space, called the Subplot, which sometimes functioned as a late night cabaret.

"He was great about having students audition," Bishop recalled. "I waited tables in the Subplot. I was sick during that time, always leaving and coming back to catch up." Bishop had minor roles in several plays before setting out on his own, first at Playwrights Horizons, where he served was literary manager and then artistic director, eventually as producing artistic director of Lincoln Center Theater, where he remains today.

The 1974-75 season would be another watershed for The American Place, as Handman and Miles responded to the pressures, old and new, that were weighing on them. For the first time, the theater began a season not with a new play, but with a revival. The Handmans had become friendly with the great humorist S. J. Perelman, whose *The Beauty Part*, written for Bert Lahr, had opened and closed during the New York City newspaper strike of December, 1962 through March, 1963.

"We thought it needed a second try," Handman says. But Perelman, who'd written for the Marx Brothers, seemed out of place in the Watergate Seventies, and the second coming of *The Beauty Part* fared no better with critics or audiences than the first. However, Perelman himself was a valuable resource to be exploited, as Handman soon discovered. While plays were lined up for the main stage, the second space was more challenging.

"We moved into the new building and there was this space, really a passageway, that we called the Subplot," Handman recalled. "First, I thought of making it a jazz cabaret. We had Daphne Hellman, the jazz harpist, in there. Then we presented stand-up comedy — J.J. Walker, Jay Leno. Then we had singers: Diane Keaton was very insecure. She kept ducking behind the curtain for words of encouragement from her boyfriend, Woody Allen, who was very shy, apologetic. And we had developed *What's a Nice Country Like You Doing in a State Like This?* there.

"I had Sid Perelman, America's outstanding humorist," Handman continued. "I talked to him about humor versus stand-up. That's when we developed the American Humorists series for the Subplot. I was talking a lot with Perelman, who had written several of the Marx Brothers movies. I started thinking about American humor and he was very erudite. He could have written a book about the origins of American humor. He mentioned George Ade. I never heard of Ade, who frequently appears in crossword puzzles. Perelman said he had started the free associational humor which then Robert Benchley picked up, and then him. Jean Shepherd had written *The America of George Ade*. Ade wrote a daily newspaper column in Chicago, and then in the teens he wrote Broadway comedies. I contacted Jean and said let's do a show where you do George Ade.

"He loved it. *Jean Shepherd and the America of George Ade* was a one-person show, no production whatsoever, Jean standing there talking."

A creative solution to a practical problem, the American Humorists series would prove to be one of The American Place's most enduring and popular contributions to the New York theater of the Seventies and Eighties, bringing a raft of performers to the awkward space while polishing the legends of some of America's greatest comic writers or giving a platform to some of its youngest and most talented ones. In the former group were shows dedicated to H. L. Mencken (*The Impossible H.L. Mencken*) and Alexander Woollcott (*Smart Alec: Alexander Woollcott at 8:40*).

"The next one was *At Sea With Benchley, Kalmar and Ruby*. Benchley was thriving in the days of transatlantic ships," recalled Handman. "We conceived it being on a ship. Then we did *Jean Shepherd Plays Jean Shepherd*. Then *We're in the Money*. I liked the idea of doing songs from the Depression. And I wanted to get in my cousin, Lou Handman and his song, `Puddinhead Jones.'"

Other highlights of the series included Sketches from Kaufman and Hart from *We're in the Money: Humor and Music of the Depression* to *Conversations with Don B*. One of the biggest hits was Jules Feiffer's *Hold Me*, which came out of acting exercises done in Handman's acting classes.

"Well, you know Feiffer was the cartoonist for the *Village Voice*," Handman recalled. "The spoken lines were very pithy, and I'd have my students perform those little scenes. I started experimenting with it. We cast Kathleen Chalfant, Paul Dooley and Geraldine Brooks. Caymichael Patten directed it in the Subplot and it became a big hit.

"Now, this is where I'm too narrowly focused. I thought it could only work in a café, not in a theater, because that was where we originated it. And here I had an empty theater all summer — and I stupidly rented another, the Westside Cabaret Theater, rather than putting it in my own theater!"

Chalfant recalls that period with a sense of amazement. She was a young actress living and working in Woodstock, New York, when she asked a friend for advice as she prepared to move to New York City. The answer was one sentence long: Find an acting teacher.

"On my 28th birthday, in 1973, I was interviewed by Wynn," says Chalfant, who would go on to win acclaim for her extraordinary performances in *Angels in America* and *Wit*. "I hadn't gone to acting school. Yet for reasons that remain unclear to me to this day, he invited me to join his class. I studied with him for two or three years.

"Wynn was — is — an astonishing teacher. He had no dogma. The thing about him teaching was that the only goal was being truthful. He didn't care how you got there, just that you got there. He was an incredible witness to what you were doing.

"He wanted you to be good and he was quite patient, but if he saw that you couldn't do it, he would encourage you to leave.

"It was an alive and fierce community. Wynn was a remarkable mentor and director. He was up for anything. I was really lucky."

The American Humorists series would provide a soapbox to such contemporary literary wits as journalist Roger

Rosenblatt, humorist Roy Blount Jr., and *New Yorker* poly-math Calvin Trillin.

"I remember walking down those stairs with Wynn to see Roy Blount," Trillin recalled, "and being very impressed with the poster. I asked Wynn, 'Did you make that poster just for Roy's show?' He told me that not only did they have a poster, but that the tickets had his name on them, too. I thought that was pretty impressive — and that I ought to do a show and have a poster as well."

Phyllis Newman was another longtime acting student of Wynn's who would get an unanticipated opportunity during that extraordinary season. Newman and her husband, the lyricist Adolph Green — who, with his writing partner Betty Comden had been responsible for such iconic New York shows as *On the Town*, *Bells Are Ringing* and *Subways Are for Sleeping* (in which Newman co-starred) — had long been part of the Handmans' extended circle. Wynn had in mind a show that would put Green and both of his partners, not to mention a significant number of their most fecund friends, to work on a sketch revue titled *Straws in the Wind.*

"The idea was Wynn's," Newman recalled one afternoon in a conversation at the Central Park aerie she has lived in for half a century. "He wanted to do a piece, or a series of pieces, about the future. He came up with the title — I don't know if it's a quote from something else, but that was the title he gave me. I'm very good at putting together a revue, that kind of thing."

To write the scenes, Handman brought in Broadway book writer Peter Stone, author Donald Barthelme and com-edy writer Marshall Brickman. To compose the music, the great Cy Coleman worked with *Hair*'s Galt MacDermot and *Godspell*'s Stephen Schwartz. It was as disparate a cast of behind-the-scenes characters as one could hope for.

Thumbing through the files she still has from the show, Newman recalled that *Straws* provided, among other things, Coleman's first work with Comden and Green, a collabora-tion that would, nearly two decades later and with Stone as librettist, produce the Tony-winning *Will Rogers Follies.*

"The material was first-rate," Newman said. "There was a song called 'Test Tube Baby — With Apologies to Stephen

Sondheim,' that was to be sung to the tune of 'Broadway Baby,' it says here, by a woman in a fetal position, perhaps in an oversize plastic test tube:

I'm just a test-tube baby / Is this any way to live?
Oh but what I would not give / to be in a womb...

It's very funny, there are verses and verses. I don't know who wrote it; it sounds like Betty and Adolph. And it wasn't in the show!"

The first published reference to *Straws in the Wind* that I could find was a tribute written for the *Times* by Coleman after Adolph Green's sudden death in 2002. The critics never got to see *Straws*.

The handsome face of young actor Richard Gere was half-hidden for Sam Shepard's monologue, *Killer's Head* (1975). (Photo by Martha Holmes.)

"The only reason it was not reviewed was because I wouldn't allow it," Newman says. "and Wynn just said, 'OK.'

"He was always there for me, quietly giving notes. There was no heat about it. Yet I was truly frightened that I hadn't made it good enough. It really tried for a lot. And now I'm sorry it wasn't reviewed. Is it too late to call the *Times*?"

The season saw Shepard's return with another double bill, of *Killer's Head* and *Action*. The first was a fantasy monologue delivered by a man strapped into an electric chair, about to be executed. It was performed by another of Handman's young students, an unknown actor named Richard Gere.

"I was in my early 20's, it must have been '70, '71 when I started studying with Wynn," Gere recalled. "I had done some theater in Provincetown. I was a singer and actor, I had long hair, was doing rock operas. Wynn wasn't coming from a clan, he was his own person. He reminds me of a history teacher I had in high school. For him the past was in the present and the future was in the present. Wynn had that quality. He was slightly mad. He would giggle with delight when something worked. He had me working on Shakespeare, *Henry V*. Shakespeare wasn't really me, it scared me. Wynn got me to stop thinking and just do it. I remember thinking, *Oh,* that's *how it's supposed to work.*

"Wynn was different in his theater than in class. In the theater, it was about the playwright, the text. At that time you want to do new plays, something exciting, and make money. I don't even remember if I read for *Killer's Head*," he continued. "I was strapped in a chair, blindfolded and shackled. It was an exercise in manifesting a person. Images kept popping into my head. I remember being in the swell of this guy's mind as he is waiting to be executed. Wynn's one note, which came to me through the director, was that he wanted to hear the text more clearly."

Phyllis Newman has her own distinct memories of studying with Handman. "I studied with him forever," she told me. "The first time I went, I knew he was it. Wynn is a man of great scruples, intelligence, and he is an honest to God intellectual. In class we did a lot of Clifford Odets. Wynn's one great note was, 'You don't speak it. There's a machine gun inside you.' It was about timing, intensity.

"He also loved directing poetry. The one he always came back to was Emily Dickinson." She started to recite:

> I'm nobody! Who are you?
> Are you nobody, too?
> Then there's a pair of us — don't tell!
> They'd banish — you know!
>
> How dreary to be somebody!
> How public like a frog
> To tell one's name the livelong day
> To an admiring bog!
>> (from Higginson, T. W. & Todd, Mabel Loomis, ed. *Poems by Emily Dickinson: Second Series*. Boston: Roberts Brothers, 1891.)

"He would have me do that as a scene," Newman said. "Not explaining it, just giving it to me and telling me to play it as a scene. I have to say it stood me in very good stead."

The final discovery to come out of that season was another writer, Jonathan Reynolds, a veteran of Eugene McCarthy's presidential campaign and various subsequent political wars. Reynolds was (and remains) a take-no-prisoners Swiftian satirist who, from the very start of his playwriting career, was unfazed by political correctness; indeed, he saw the embarrassment of the politically correct and the dismantlement of political correctness as the highest objective of the comic playwright's art. His first produced work was a double bill of thematically disparate but intellectually joined comedies: *Rubbers* and *Yanks 3 Detroit 0 Top of the Seventh.*

Rubbers is set in the chambers of an unnamed state legislature, where a female member is trying to introduce a bill that would permit the open display and sale of condoms. Yes, it was a quainter time; she is confronted not only with stupider and stupider argument and obfuscation by her male colleagues, but several of them are literally represented by life-size dummies.

Yanks 3 predated the movie *Bull Durham* by more than a decade. It centered on a Yankees pitcher whose best days are behind him as he experiences a crisis — no, a meltdown — of confidence on the mound while struggling to maintain a possible perfect game in the face of internal demons messing with his brain, diminishing power in his arm and the relentless heckling of the opposing team.

"Jonathan Reynolds knew Hal Prince and wanted him to direct," Handman recalls. "Hal began casting but we hadn't come to an agreement. I was uncomfortable. I was never able to conclude the negotiation with Prince, maybe because in my heart I didn't want it. In his book, *Wrestling with Gravy*, Jonathan quotes Hal saying I am the only person who ever fired him. But that's not really the case. Our negotiation ended, but he never forgot it."

"Well, I must say, *I* thought he fired Hal, and I think that's just his modest way of remembering it," Reynolds told me over lunch one day. "My first cousin was Lee Remick, who was enthusiastic about *Yanks 3 Detroit 0 Top of the Seventh* and sent it to Steve Sondheim. Weeks (possibly months) went by, and out of the blue I got a call from Steve in which he said very flattering things, winding up with `I'd like to send this to Hal Prince.' Hal responded enthusiastically. At the time, he predicted that a play would essentially try out at a not-for-profit (though it wouldn't be called a tryout), and, if well-received, would move to Broadway. That of course is now the flight plan for almost everything.

"One of the aspects of Wynn firing Hal was that Hal's designers — Franne and Eugene Lee, then married — predicted a budget of $25,000, whereas Wynn thought $2,500 was excessive."

Ultimately, the double-bill was deftly staged by Alan Arkin with wit and an astonishing economy of gesture that played brilliantly against — and thus emphasized — the extravagance of the language. The pitcher, Bronkowski, was played in a career-making performance by Tony LoBianco. As had so often been the case, the critics knew something interesting was unfolding on the stage, but they weren't quite sure what it was: "What author Reynolds needs is more event and less effortfulness," wrote Kerr in the Sunday *Times*. On the other hand, former Yankees pitcher turned best-selling baseball memoirist Jim Bouton got it.

In 1975 Jonathan Reynolds gave The American Place another hit with the double bill of *Rubbers* and *Yanks 3 Detroit 0 Top of the Seventh* with Tony LoBianco. (Photo by Martha Holmes.)

"That's *exactly* what happens to us," he said after seeing the play. "Those things go through our minds all the time."

And it took a *Times* sports columnist, Murray Chass, to articulate what the audiences were getting.

"Bronkowski, who could be any man in any profession trying to hang on to what he has, is 36 years old, married, the father of two boys and the owner of a rambling Victorian house in Roslyn, a 1966 Lincoln, a fast-food franchise and an off-season public relations job with Connecticut Federal. He also has an affair going with a groupie from Texas, Donna Luna Donna, and he's afraid he'll lose her and some of his other possessions if he doesn't pitch the perfect game." Chass cut through the raucous, ragged-edged symbolism and saw the everyman beneath.

So did subscribers, who packed the theater for its entire run and forced an extension that became the first American Place Theatre show to sell tickets to clamoring non-subscribers. *Rubbers/Yanks* was a significant commercial hit — in *New York* magazine, the famously difficult-to-please John Simon called it the funniest play of the season, and while it provided an unprecedented opportunity to sign up new subscribers, it also embodied, in some respects, the adage be careful what you wish for. As Mac Lowry had warned Handman and Lanier a decade earlier when sending the initial Ford Foundation support their way, The American Place was not supposed to be in the business of box office success; that was for commercial producers. It was to be in the business of developing talent and bringing audiences along a journey of discovery. But the move east had brought with it increased pressure — from the board, from the press, from subscribers — on Handman and Miles to fill those 348 seats night after night. *The Karl Marx Play* wasn't going to do that. *Rubbers/Yanks* did.

"*Rubbers/Yanks* had a huge cast," Handman recalled. "We had a guy selling subscriptions in the lobby, a handsome guy, selling like crazy. 10,000 was the height of our subscribers." But what were all those new subscribers signing up for? The next *Harry, Noon and Night* or the next *Yanks 3 Detroit 0 Top of the Seventh*? The answer to that question would determine the long-term success or failure of Wynn Handman's dream.

"I didn't produce *Rubbers/Yanks* to sell tickets," Handman says. "I did it because it was *talented*. Of course, we did end up selling a lot of subscriptions in the intermission."

The same spring that gave birth to *Rubbers/Yanks* at The American Place saw a similar phenomenon occur downtown at Joe Papp's Public Theater: Michael Bennett, Broadway baby and protégé of Hal Prince and Stephen Sondheim, unveiled *A Chorus Line*, his first musical as sole director and choreographer. It wasn't exactly the revolution Papp had spoken of when he took over the theaters at Lincoln Center, but it was revolutionary nonetheless, an audience-rousing show that managed to obliterate the conventions of the backstage musical while paying scrupulous homage to them at the same time, a show that appeared to defy sentiment while exploiting, even wallowing in it.

It's impossible to understate the impact *A Chorus Line* had on the theater of the mid-'70s and beyond: When the show moved uptown to the Shubert Theater, it single-handedly reversed the plummeting fortunes of Broadway. The show swept the Tony Awards, won the Pulitzer Prize for Drama and restored faith in the efficacy of the American musical (at least until *Evita* announced the British invasion of Broadway four years later).

Equally important is the impact *A Chorus Line* would have on the nonprofit theater. Unlike London, whose great companies, the National Theatre and the Royal Shakespeare Company, were heavily underwritten through public subsidy, the U.S. remained in the Dark Ages with respect to the formulation of a national culture policy. It was more akin to the Renaissance, for the American model remained everyone-for-himself and was chiefly dependent on the largesse of private patrons. The National Endowment for the Arts and its counterparts in state governments never promulgated a coherent set of principles, probably because the idea of public subsidy remains antithetical in a market-driven society. So while *A Chorus Line* had been developed with the help of the Shakespeare Festival's minuscule public funding, its success in the commercial marketplace of Broadway did more for the Public Theater than decades of NEA grants. By the time it ended its record-breaking run in April, 1990 after 6,137 performances, the show had not only made its creators wealthy beyond their wildest dreams, but it had poured nearly $38 million into the New York Shakespeare Festival's coffers, making it the most solvent nonprofit cultural institution in the country.

And the most envied. Suddenly every nonprofit theater was looking for the next *A Chorus Line* and that, of course, would have a significant distorting impact on the artistic direction those theaters would take. While the Wynn Handmans and Ellen Stewarts stayed the course, looking for new writers and new material, other theaters were torn between their artistic mission and the need for box-office success in the light of diminishing public support that put them at the mercy of producers offering seed money — "enhancement funds" is the preferred euphemism — to develop shows with commercial potential. It's a creative schism that has only grown worse in the intervening years and continues to be the subject of one of the most hotly debated issues in the performing arts.

For several more seasons, The American Place attracted new writers while continuing to see its veterans grow. Steve Tesich returned with *Gorky*, in 1975-'76, and then *Passing Game* in '77-'78 and then *Touching Bottom* in '78-79. In 1977, Ribman's most accessible play, *Cold Storage*, about a battle of wits between two old men dying of cancer, won over the critics and within the year moved to Broadway, though without the profit participation of The American Place. And one star, Martin Balsam, was not enough; by the time it transferred, *Cold Storage* had added Len Cariou to the cast. It has become a staple of the repertory, Ribman said, still performed all over the country.

That season also saw Marian Seldes return, in another of the great early leading performances of her career, the title role in Jeff Wanshel's loopy vaudeville romance, *Isadora Duncan Sleeps with the Russian Navy*, a play that prompted Walter Kerr to mutter (rather loudly, as he was doing so in the pages of the Sunday *Times)*: "Always remember, the Bastille fell. The American Place can fall, too."

"I can remember walking down a street in New York and bumping into Wynn and he said, `I have a play about Isadora Duncan I want you to do,'" Seldes recalls. "I didn't like that title *ever*, but I loved the fact that almost every line the character said was written by her. The writer of the play, Jeff Wanshel, had workshopped it with Meryl Streep, who was later unavailable to continue with it. He preferred her. He didn't like me. I had never been in a situation where I was the disappointing one, and I didn't want to let Wynn down. I'd had a career of playing supporting parts, and for Wynn I played the central part and — ha ha! — I just have to say to you I prefer playing the part that the play is about. You have the greater responsibility and the sense that if you don't have the variety to make it interesting, it can collapse. I never felt at The American Place it was a sense of success that you were doing it for. That wasn't the point, darling. The point was to do the work on the script as diligently as possible."

Shepard returned, as well, this time with *Seduced*, a full-length riff on the life of Howard Hughes, an at times moving, at times hilarious meditation on American themes (which all of Shepard's plays were, though rarely with such a high-profile focal point). The show starred Rip Torn as Henry Hackamore, and featured Jill Haworth, a British actress who had originated the role of Sally Bowles in the Broadway debut of *Cabaret*. Although she never returned to Broadway after playing Sally for two years, Haworth did two shows at the American Place — *Seduced* and Jonathan Reynolds's *Tunnel Fever*.

Shepard missed the *gemütlich* atmosphere at St. Clements, and Torn proved to be as eccentric as the man he was playing, according to the playwright.

"It was an entirely different theater, concrete, it had a whole different feeling, which I didn't like, a different feeling than the old American Place," Shepard recalls. "I really didn't like the theater physically, it was a big concrete slab, and I didn't think the play fit there, it was so wide. It seemed big, and cold. Concrete is the worst environment for a play. I thought it had bad acoustics.

In 1979 Shepard returned to The American Place again with
Seduced, his rumination on Howard Hughes,
starring Rip Torn and Pamela Reed. (Photo by Martha Holmes.)

"Rip Torn wanted the heat turned off in the theater, so everyone was freezin' their asses off," he continued. "I wasn't around, I was in California. It's one of those plays I should have spent more time with. It's not fulfilled. I should have spent more time with it, but I was always on to the next thing. Missed opportunity."

Most of the fundraising responsibilities had fallen to Julia Miles, who had become adept at finding money to underwrite plays or series with specific themes. The American Place had always reached out to women writers, as it had with writers of color, providing them a place at the table. Among the other highlights of the previous seasons had been the productions of Maria Irene Fornes's *Fefu and Her Friends*, an early example of environmental or site-specific theater in which audience members were shuttled among a series of rooms where different scenes unfolded; Elaine Jackson's *Cockfight*, and, of course, plays by Joyce Carol Oates and Rochelle Owens.

"*Fefu and Her Friends* was a seminal play," Handman recalls. "My literary manager, Bonnie Marranca, was wild about it. She saw it in somebody's apartment in the Village, where it ran for 12 performances. I saw it and decided to do it. There was something ineffable about the women in that play. Irene calls it 'distilled naturalism.'

Fefu and Her Friends, in 1978, brought playwright Maria Irene Fornes (standing at center) to the uptown audience. (Photo by Martha Holmes.)

"*Fefu* appealed more to women than to men. Women are more aware of relationships and this was about women relating to each other. Women left to themselves are going to write different plays than men. They're more about nesting, creating wombs, less filled with dramatic tension. *Fefu* really had no plot, no conflict. It was a woman writing about women, and it had very strong images because Irene had started as a painter. Richard Eder in the *Times* got it, and he gave it an insightful review."

Miles saw in *Fefu and Her Friends* an opportunity to go further. The same season that saw the productions of *Seduced* and Tesich's *Touching Bottom* also saw the introduction of the Women's Project, a series of studio productions of work by women writers, for which Miles had secured a Ford Foundation pilot project grant. The first offering of the Women's Project was *Choices*, a one-woman show conceived by writer Patricia Bosworth that drew from the writings of a wide range of women, from Colette to Joan Didion.

"The production explores the choices that women have," Miles said at the time, adding, "Hopefully, there are more of those choices and women are more definite about what they are."

Choices ran in December, 1978 and was followed by other works, including Lavonne Mueller's *Warriors From a Long Childhood,* and *Letters Home*, a full-length dramatization of the poet Sylvia Plath's letters to her mother.

Almost from the beginning, the Women's Project was established as Julia Miles's fiefdom and responsibility.

"It was a time when women were coming into their own," she recalled. "Wynn read some of the plays, but I chose what we produced. We have very similar taste — we wanted to do plays that had something to say."

By the summer of 1979 The American Place, once virtually alone in its mission, now had a lot of competition. The long winter of the Seventies had come to an end with the flourishing of Off Broadway theaters catering to every taste. The Manhattan Theater Club had found it's *A Chorus Line* in *Ain't Misbehavin'*, a musical revue based on the songs of Fats Waller that had begun life in its tiny patrons' lounge and transferred to a hugely successful Broadway run.

"I was there for the first day of the Women's Project," André Bishop recalls. "Wynn and Bobbie were buoyant with enthusiasm, so writer-oriented." Bishop soon moved on to Playwrights Horizons, but didn't cut his ties with his mentor.

"At Playwrights Horizons I co-produced two shows with Wynn, Ron Ribman's *Buck* and Ted Talley's *Terra Nova,*" Bishop says. Choosing his words carefully he continues, his voice now tinged with regret.

"The sadness I feel about Wynn, which I say with admiration and love — he was a *seminal* figure — is that after a certain period, he isolated himself from the theater," Bishop says. "He rarely went to the theater. In my thirteen years at Playwrights Horizons, I think he came maybe twice. The whole movement he helped start overtook him. He didn't keep up his board, which, like it or not you have to do."

Bishop also pointed out what had become obvious to most observers of The American Place: The space at 111 West Forty-sixth Street exacerbated old problems and brought new ones.

"The new building was a blessing and a curse," he said. "It was a boutique theater with a narrow and specific view. To stay afloat became harder and harder. You couldn't stay open with just a Ford grant."

A *Times* report from July 1979 sent the first signals that not all was well at The American Place. Announcing the upcoming season, it noted that the theater "has had its difficulties, as anything dedicated to the new and experimental must..."

Almost everything on the upcoming schedule was divvied up among the different American Place programs, whether the American Humorists' series or the Women's Project. And if Handman and Miles were going to have to host other productions to help pay the bills, then at least they were going to find work that reflected the values of The American Place. That certainly was the case with Spalding Gray and Elizabeth LeCompte's sad, searing memory play, *Rumstick Road*, which had been developed downtown by the nascent Wooster Group but was given its first wider audience from the stage at 111 West Forty-sixth Street.

"I didn't do *Rumstick Road* because I didn't have anything else," Handman insists. "I did it because I thought it was a masterpiece. I couldn't get over it. It's like a fantastic painter did it. It's a work of genius."

Handman acknowledges that the greater the pressure to become more populist, to hire stars, the greater his determination to resist grew.

"In the '70s, I saw what was happening. I'm never part of a scene, I'm a maverick, I guess. I resist being put together with someone," he says. "My nature is to be *too* narrowly focused. I was in a period where the audience was diminishing. There was a proliferation of theaters doing work that was more popular. The American Place Theatre had a serious intellectual aura, but my audiences were no longer around.

Marian Seldes returned in the title role of Jeff Wanshel's loopy *Isadora Duncan Sleeps With the Russian Navy* (1977). Photo by Martha Holmes.

"I shied away from popularity — maybe a little too much," he admits. "My work did not lead to expanding audiences. I couldn't do middle-brow work, I'm not out to do hits. I'm delinquent. I don't keep up relationships, which really hurt the fundraising. Sam Shepard knew my dedication to writers, my function was to serve them. Then I got bitter when I had to start getting names to fill the theater.

119

"And I did get rather bitter about the subscription situation. The competition came in — Manhattan Theatre Club, Playwrights Horizons — with a much broader net. I've never been the 'big net' person, I'm always fishing for the one big fish. They had hits that let them do the kinds of plays I should be doing. I was too narrowly focused. I wouldn't do *Sylvia* or *Driving Miss Daisy* or *Frankie and Johnny in the Clair de Lune*. I'm not needed for that."

Marian Seldes. (Photo by Jeremy Gerard.)

No, Handman was needed for plays like *The Cannibals* and *La Turista* and *Who's Got His Own*. Uncompromising works that challenged nearly everything that made an audience member comfortable. After Kerr's dismissal of *Isadora Duncan Sleeps with the Russian Navy*, Handman had offered up an eloquent defense in the critics home turf, the pages of the *Times*:

"There is a litany derived from hundreds of post-play discussions at The American Place and countless reviews of new writing by American playwrights. It goes like this: 'I can't identify with the characters"; 'I can't follow the story'; 'I wasn't moved'; 'I don't know the author's point of view'; 'There's no resolution'; 'What's the theme?'; 'What does it all mean?' These are responses to plays by writers whose works reflect a chaotic world, its fragmentation, ambiguity, terror, and random, rapid, directionless change," Handman wrote, noting that Clive Barnes himself had recently recanted his first, negative response to Fernando Arrabal's *The Architect and the Emperor of Assyria* after a second viewing some years later gave him a completely different impression and he declared it a modern classic.

Gloria LeRoy and Kevin O'Connor starred in Ron Tavel's musical
drama, *Boy on a Straight-Back Chair* (1969) ,
which won an Obie Award. (Photo by Martha Holmes.)

"I have suggested to the puzzled in the audiences at post-
play discussions that they let themselves be available to the new
worlds of these plays," Handman implored the *Times*'s readers.
"Do not work at finding meanings, let it happen to you, let the
spray play on you, let the images soak in, let yourself move into
a new space. Have room for the contemporary writers."

But one thing that did not change was the hostility of many
critics, especially Kerr, to what was happening on The American
Place Theatre stages. Kerr was as withering in his assessment of
the Women's Project as he had been about *Isadora Duncan*.

"All of the surprises in *Letters Home* are sharp disappoint-
ments," he wrote, and that was just the lead. The play lacked
the startling imagery of Plath's poetry, Kerr complained, "as
everything else at The American Place goes sadly wrong."

121

CHAPTER SEVEN:
HITS, RUNS, ERRORS

*'Drinking in America' caught both Wynn and me by
surprise. All of a sudden we had this hit on our hands.*
Eric Bogosian, actor and playwright

IN NOVEMBER, 1980, JULIA MILES made an excruci-
ating decision. A commercial production of a new children's
musical, Maurice Sendak and Carole King's *Really Rosie*,
needed a bigger theater. Miles was faced with a financial
crisis: For the first time, The American Place had ended its
previous season with a deficit — a rather large deficit, at
$75,000 — that it couldn't make up, and the money for the
current season was still not in place. Miles pushed Handman
and The American Place board to offer the main stage as a
rental to the producers of *Really Rosie*. Ironically, the show
had originated as a rental at another seminal nonprofit theater
in a financial bind, the Chelsea Theater Center, which had
been forced to cancel its season for lack of funds.

"The financial crunch is just horrendous," Miles said at
the time. "The foundations have pulled back from nonprofit
theater. We've always been able to handle our deficit until
last year. We're working with a skeleton staff. The one thing
we can do to get money in here is to rent the building."

The season was hardly a washout, however. For one
thing, the Women's Project was attracting new writers and
strong casts; the highlight of the season was Emily Mann's
Still Life, a remarkable Vietnam play in which John Spen-

cer played a veteran plagued with post-traumatic stress syndrome, and its impact on his wife, played by Mary Mc-Donnell, and his mistress, played by Timothy Near. Mann was a newcomer experimenting with testimonial theater in a documentary format — in *Still Life* the three characters sat at a table and rarely interacted with each other — that built in power to an extraordinary climax (all of it missed by Barnes's recent replacement at the *Times*, Frank Rich, whose blistering dismissal of the play made Kerr's reviews seem like fan mail by comparison).

The provocatively posed Annette Kurek in W.D.Snodgrass's *The Fuehrer Bunker* (1981). (Photo by Martha Holmes)

With *Really Rosie* occupying the main stage, *Still Life* had been crammed into the Subplot, unable to take advantage of the good reviews it did manage to get in papers like the *Soho Weekly News*.

The season ended literally with a bang: the poet W.D. Snodgrass this time returned to The American Place as playwright with *The Fuehrer Bunker*, depicting the final hours of Hitler, Eva Braun and their cohorts.

"The theater's flexibility was most important for *The Fuehrer Bunker*," Handman recalls. "I wanted to recreate the feeling of the bunker. The German designer was a genius. There was a bombed-out area, detritus of the war. It looked incredible. Clive Barnes was at the *Post* by then and the question was, where do you put critics? Clive had a reputation for falling asleep at shows. So I put him next to Eva Braun, who was in her underwear, to keep him awake. He loved her. He gave her a *great* review."

The '80s saw the continuation of both the American Humorists' series and the Women's Project. On the main stage in the spring of 1982, Bill Irwin, a brilliant physical comedian from San Francisco who'd trained in classical theater and with the avant-garde comedy troupe Pickle Family Circus, brought his astonishing, and astonishingly funny show, *The Regard of Flight*, to The American Place. He'd been brought to Handman's attention by Julie Taymor, who would go on win fame as the director of *The Lion King* and *Spider-Man: Turn Off the Dark*. As with so many artists who encountered Handman, Irwin got more than he expected out of the relationship.

"I did some pieces in the late 70's, early 80's at Dance Theatre Workshop — clown pieces for modern dance audiences, stuff within the "New Vaudeville" bailiwick, though I've never liked that term," Irwin recalled. "Not sure how Wynn and I met, but he showed me The American Place. I was a provincial, if not a straight-out hick, and I thought what he was discussing with me was pretty much like a booking, of the sort I'd done downtown, or regionally, or in festivals in Europe — what, a weekend or two, maybe."

"I toured the theater with Doug Skinner, my long time colleague and collaborator, and his Italian girlfriend of the time,"

Irwin continues. "Skinner was forever conquering foreign women's hearts, and when we did brief European tours — in the days long before the Euro — he'd always then return with a young woman, or would soon be visited by one. This was the delightful Margarita, and she said to us, as we walked away from meeting Wynn and seeing the theater, '*Beel*, I think in this theater, they will pay LOTS of money,' and both Skinner and I said, 'No, I don't think so,' though why, I can't remember. Though in many ways — in relative terms at least and in the currency of *gift*, and *opportunity*, this turned out to be true.

Bill Irwin, a leading performer in the New Vaudeville movement, dazzled audiences with *The Regard of Flight* (1982). (Photo by Martha Holmes.)

"Wynn came to San Francisco. I didn't appreciate what a thing that was — what a deal, what a potential *life-changer* that was — or how much Wynn was extending himself. He came out to see something that we were doing — a piece titled *The Regard of Flight* (though I'd used that title, or variants, before). It was an unfinished and sort of ungainly attempt at an amalgamation of material.

"My main memory of Wynn was his friendliness, and his easy gregariousness, and his pride of ownership as he showed us around. The lobby was full of pictures of Dustin Hoffman and past productions. I remember well the pay phone in that lobby, because the place got to be a home to me in the next several months."

Bill Irwin today, now a Broadway and Hollywood regular.
(Photo by Jeremy Gerard.)

Regard was an inspired work of comic inventiveness (indeed, two years later, Irwin would be awarded the first Mac-Arthur Foundation "genius grant" to go to a performing artist) that took classic comedic genres — commedia dell'arte, mime, burlesque, clowning — and turned them on their heads or inside out, to hilarious effect. It was one of the first examples of meta-theater—theater that self-consciously made fun of itself. Both the *Times*'s daily critic, Mel Gussow, and the usually antagonistic Kerr, on Sunday, offered whole-hearted approval.

"Mr. Irwin, who is now making a delectable shambles of the new venture at The American Place," Kerr wrote, "is young, unruly, unpainted (no clown-white), able to stand not upon his head but upon his hat, given to juggling and able to impersonate the gyrations of a rock star so wholeheartedly that he turns himself into a strobe light before he's done. If Mr. Irwin is still in the process of finding himself, he is already very funny."

Irwin recalls it as a defining experience, in which he very suddenly emerged from the wings into the New York spotlight, with everything that implied: fame, money, acclaim, unanticipated opportunities. Until then, he'd been a novice; now he was in the full flush of stardom.

"Wynn somehow shepherded me through the process of mounting an Off-Broadway piece, without my ever really catching on to what that meant or what we were doing," he recalled. "Being an out-of-towner and a clown, I really had no idea. This was a function both of my lack of knowledge, and his slightly ethereal mode, I think. He connected me with David Jenkins, who did a wonderful set conception and design just from descriptions of the action (there was *no* script). Most important to me — though it cost Wynn nothing and was just an in-house assignment — was that he introduced me to Nancy Harrington, the resident stage manager. I had no idea what a stage manager really was, and remember thinking that I hoped she wasn't going to get in the way of things. Nancy became one of the most important people in my life.

"And, *very* important, and something that *did* cost Wynn money, was that he put us in rehearsal, on the stage, for a week or two. That's where the piece, *The Regard of Flight*, the Off-Broadway show, was really shaped. Wynn as I recall was around occasionally, but engaged upstairs and then laughed hard when we showed him anything. The venue was Midtown Theater District — but the approach was almost collegiate, experimental. I remember coming up with an ending that involved driving a stake into the heart of the critic character, and showing this to Wynn and him laughing really hard. We knew we had something, with him laughing. He was the perfect producer.

The success of Eric Bogosian's one-man show
Drinking in America nearly overwhelmed The American Place.
(Photo by Martha Holmes.)

"Wynn got us open and got us reviewed. He *never* liked to pay for much advertising. He seemed to have a special aversion, as I recall, to paying anything to the *Village Voice*. What else? Wynn was such a supportive — but low-key — man of the theater. Lord, how long ago it was. I owe Wynn a great, great, *great* deal and thinking back on this chagrins me more than a little. I was young, and the young never get this."

Genius of a different sort came into the picture not long after.

"I got to New York in '75, worked at Chelsea Theater Center, I'd go to The American Place," recalls monologist and playwright Eric Bogosian. "The most memorable performance I saw was Richard Gere in Sam Shepard's *Killer's Head*, although I didn't realize at the time that it was a seminal performance for me, for what I do. He was jumping out of his seat. It was electric and a little surreal. One of the first pieces I did, I realized I was stealing from *Killer's Head*."

In 1982, Bogosian had performed his first solo piece, *Funhouse*, at the Public Theater. During that time, he stopped drinking and doing drugs, and although he didn't plan it, he wrote another full-length monologue, *Drinking in America*. But Papp wasn't interested in following up a monologue with a monologue.

"I was moping around town," Bogosian says. "I ran into [*Village Voice* senior critic] Michael Feingold, who asked, 'When are you going to do another solo show?' I told him I had one but that Joe didn't want it, and he said I should do it at The American Place. He asked Wynn to see me. It was 1985. I was really at my highest level of hot-headed-dom . I had an appointment with Wynn. Maybe 15 minutes went by; I could see him on the phone, so I started to walk out. He came out and said, 'Where are you going?' I told him what I was doing. He said he was interested but thought I had not investigated the character. He wanted to direct me. Bill Irwin had gone to Oberlin, like me, and had a huge hit with *Regard of Flight*. It was a chance to work with a great teacher. I remember Wynn watching me. He was insightful. I think I was a little bit of a mystery to him. He basically asked questions specific to the character, like 'Who is this guy?' 'Where does he come from?' or my favorite, which I had never considered before with this monologue work, 'What's his name?' "

Drinking in America earned the best reviews The American Place had gotten in years, for both Bogosian and Handman, who was finally getting his due as a director who took the raw material of both actor and text and built them into something bigger than either could be alone.

"There are few theatrical experiences more exhilarating than watching a talented young artist fulfill his promise," Rich began his *Times* review. "That experience is now to be had at

The American Place Theater, where the performer Eric Bogo-sian, a downtown fixture for almost a decade, has put together an airtight 80-minute show in which his gifts for acting and social satire collide to their most incendiary effect yet.

"In what may be the tour-de-force of *Drinking in America*, a blue-collar hood regales a buddy with an account of an all-night booze-and-acid binge of partying that escalated into a violent crime spree. The events are described in vivid subliterate ver-nacular, and, like a car pile-up on a highway, they are grotesquely slapstick. But even as we laugh, we are terrified by the cruelty of a hooligan whose manic giggles and cracker-barrel storytelling style cannot hide a complete absence of conscience. If there are several such high points in *Drinking in America,* there are no real valleys. Whether due to experience or to the added presence of the director Wynn Handman, Mr. Bogosian has for the first time edited his material and his performance to the quick. *Drinking in America* rarely slows down, and it has been cohesively as-sembled to achieve a cumulative effect."

Demands for tickets quickly overwhelmed The American Place's ability to handle them.

"*Drinking in America* caught both Wynn and me by sur-prise," Bogosian recalls. "All of a sudden, we had this hit on our hands. He paid me and I was making more than I ever had in my life. One night I was throwing myself so violently on the stage my forehead hit the floor. Wynn took me to Roosevelt Hospital. We forgot there was an audience there waiting for me to continue. No one ever sent them home. We just forgot.

"Wynn was a totally foreign character to me, a guy who was part of the big New York City scene. I had had no expe-rience of uptown theater, Elaine's, all the successful lefties Wynn knew, particularly Norman Lear, so I was kind of agog. I guess my big surprise was that he was a real family guy. I figured any tall, good-looking guy like him would be a womanizing drunk. Now, perhaps he is, I don't know. I just remember that at the time he doted on his wife and daughters and was very proud of them and I liked this.

"Within twelve months of meeting Wynn, I would be rocketed into the real Hollywood world and have some real characters with whom to compare him," Bogosian continued. "But at that time, he was basically a very powerful father-figure, like Joe Papp was to me. I was still wet behind the ears. Wynn was like a movie star. He has tremendous presence, like John Wayne or something, tall, hale. He would tell me tales of Dustin Hoffman. Now I hear from students he tells them stories about me."

A similar kind of lightning would strike a few years later when another monologuist came into Handman's world.

John Leguizamo continues to write solo shows based on characters from his life, while having a major Hollywood career. (Photo by Jeremy Gerard.)

"John Leguizamo came to my class." says Handeman. He brought in a character, and then another. He didn't just bring them in in an embryonic state, he had costumes, they were completely developed. He had all these characters. We developed the show, called it *Mambo Mouth*. Peter Askin directed. John was wonderful." *Mambo Mouth*, too, was introduced in the Subplot space before transferring to a long commercial run in the wake of great reviews. But it was growing ever more difficult to keep the theater open."

Although the Women's Project continued to present plays at The American Place, by the mid-80s it was running as a separate operation. Miles was looking for outside support and in 1983 found it with backers Anne Wilder, Douglas F. Goodman and Rosie Sarnoff, who financed the development of a *A...My Name Is* Alice, a serio-comic proto-feminist musical review conceived by directors Joan Micklin Silver and Julianne Boyd. Pieces were contributed by writers and composers including Lucy Simon, Winnie Holtzman, Anne Meara, David Zippel, Susan Birkenhead and the team of Marta Kaufman and David Crane.

John Malkovich rehearses Sam Shepard's *States of Shock* with the playwright (1991). (Photo by Martha Holmes.)

After a brief run downtown at the Village Gate, the show opened in the Subplot in February, 1984 for a two-week run. After enthusiastic notices (Frank Rich's *Times* review began, "*A...My Name Is Alice* is the less-than-inspiring title of a delightful new musical revue in the cellar of the American Place Theater. And when I say cellar, I'm not exaggerating. *Alice* is being performed in a small and airless room, reached by elevator. The show has few production values, odd curtain times and only a piano for a band. It's amazing how little any of that matters, however, when there's fresh talent on display almost everywhere you look."), the show returned to Greenwich Village, where it ran for more than a year and spawned a mini-franchise of sequels.

In 1986 Miles left The American Place, after nearly two decades, and set up the Women's Project and Productions as an independent producing company.

"My subscription audience was pathetic," Handman admits. "I had a theater I was no longer able to fill."

The problem became circular: With other, more popular theaters to choose from, The American Place no longer was a top choice for agents placing scripts by up-and-coming writers. Talent attracts talent; once the industry loses faith that its best people will get the best showcase, it becomes harder and harder to attract other talent, and thus audiences.

"Wynn lost the confidence of the agents," says a prominent agent who had watched the fortunes of The American Place change for the worse during those years. "They didn't think they would get a first-class production any more. The theater was looking shabby. It was no longer a pleasant place to come to."

Ron Ribman blames the atmosphere of producing in general. After the initial frenzy of activity in the Sixties, foundations had begun to alter their priorities, especially as the recession of the Seventies placed higher demands on acutely affected social services. And while *A Chorus Line* was great for the health of Joe Papp's theater, it set up unrealistic expectations for the rest of the nonprofits. Audiences too, were turning their backs on demanding work of the sort that defined The American Place.

"Today, if you don't have a star, you might as well throw in the towel," Ribman says. "In 1991 I had a show at the Pasadena Playhouse with no star. We couldn't get anyone inside the theater. I think this has hurt Wynn's heart." The situation became so fraught that it led to a split between Handman and Ribman that lasted more than a decade.

"We had our falling out in '94," Ribman said. "He optioned my play *Turkish Favors*. We had a reading. *Turkish Favors* is set during World War II. It's a comedy drama about a famous European actress and her hat-manufacturing husband, and their struggle to keep their daughter alive. It's totally a work of fiction.

"Wynn felt he needed a star. He had the money and we got Amy Irving, and I'm overjoyed — and then he said he *didn't* have the money, he had to spend it on something else. I blew my stack. He blew his stack. This would not have happened when he was 35. I felt bad for him. Year by year he was pushed out on the periphery. Things became more and more difficult. The theater was going under."

In fact, the two hadn't spoken until I tracked Ribman down in West Texas for this book. Both felt they were long overdue for a reconciliation.

"Wynn, we often went to their house, we were as close... I don't know," Ribman says. "There's a Wynn Handman I don't know at all. There's a certain distance that he keeps. But he's a very sweet, dear guy. He deserved a helluva lot more recognition."

The 1990s were not, of course, without their own share of high points for The American Place, despite the financial struggles. In 1991, Sam Shepard returned with his first work in six years, *States of Shock*, a remarkable antiwar play — it was during the Persian Gulf war — that starred John Malkovich in another ferocious performance.

"*States of Shock* has a furious, staccato energy," I wrote in my *Variety* review, "barely contained in John Malkovich's fevered performance...It is more piercing and more concise than the rambling, overrated *Lie of the Mind*. The new play has more in common with Shepard's two great works of the '70s, *Curse of the Starving Class* and *Buried Child* and reaffirms Shepard's status as a master conjurer of the images and icons, dreams and ambitions that dog Americans and infuriate the rest of the world. It is an unsettling vision, as ugly in its way as *Miss Saigon* but infinitely more seductive."

The same year, Shepard's mentor and sometime collaborator, Joseph Chaikin, collaborated with another figure from their early downtown years, playwright Jean-Claude van Itallie, on two shows: *The War in Heaven* and *Struck Dumb*.

Downtown puppeteer Theodora Skipitares' *The Radiant City* was a haunting meditation on Robert Moses long before it was fashionable to revisit the legendary power broker's complicated legacy. Public radio journalist John Hockenberry, under Handman's intense tutelage, produced a powerfully moving solo piece, *Spoke Man*, about his life from age 19, when an automobile accident left him paralyzed from the chest down and dependent on a wheelchair to get around.

Author and public radio commentator John Hockenberry performed his solo show, *Spoke Man* (1996). (Photo by Martha Holmes.)

"I continued to want The American Place to serve great talents who weren't writing for the theater," Handman says. "John Hockenberry is not a playwright but a very gifted, talented, intelligent man, as well as a paraplegic. He was well-known as a journalist for National Public Radio. He came to me because I'd worked with Roger Rosenblatt. His agent, Gloria Loomis, said, 'Well you ought to get to know John Hockenberry.'

"So I met with John and we developed his piece. He approached it with not great confidence, and a lot of his instincts were not right for the drama. But certain metaphors he has, like Olympic Jumpers, were just so big for him. We made a special set, it had curves and ramps and the background was a beautiful piece of abstract art. He just came swooping in and around. I had Art Tatum recordings playing behind him: the blind jazz piano virtuoso behind the virtuoso of the wheelchair."

"*Spoke Man* is a bit like Brian Friel's *Molly Sweeney*: the past remains past, as it must when it's presented as events recollected in monologues," wrote Vincent Canby in the *Times*. "The drama depends entirely on the narrator. Mr. Hockenberry is very good, but carries a nearly impossible burden. He must play himself every night and make fresh the dramatic events he himself remembered. Where does the man leave off and the actor take over? It's strange theater, but theater of a kind we are seeing with increasing frequency these days. In most other instances, usually the stories of performers, the results have been self-congratulatory freak show: the theater's minimal equivalent to the television docudrama in which Joan Rivers plays herself getting over her husband's suicide. *Spoke Man* is something else. As directed by Wynn Handman, it's serious and, in its own mild way, entertaining, but I'm not sure it's theater." Well, few others who saw the show shared any such reservation about whether or not it qualified as theater.

Spoke Man was not part of the American Humorist series, but a return to the mainstage and the company's patented orneriness about tacking against the mainstream winds.

"Now we come to *The Vi-Ton-Ka Medicine Show*, which was absolutely unique, and done at the last time you could possibly do it," Handman says. "I had a folklorist who went all over the country to find people who had acted in medicine shows, which really were precursors of what radio and television would come to be, because they were free entertainment, they made their money by selling this elixir, which was some phony concoction with a little bit of alcohol and flavoring.

"The key person there was the Doc, who does the spiel to sell it. These people who didn't know each other, came from the south, the west, Texas, we put together the show, I got along great with these people. There was Walking Mary McClain, a blues singer, the Hired Hands, a real country

137

group. We had a sharpshooter and a bullwhip guy — and we had a very brave intern who got shot at and near-whipped and who later went to the Yale Drama School. We made the elixir — of course, we didn't use alcohol — we had the bottles, we sold it, with boxes of candy.

"We put all of them up at the Wentworth Hotel. We had a cook, these people were not going to eat in New York restaurants, it was like an old folks home over at the Wentworth. He cooked them grits for lunch and then supper before the show. It ran maybe a month. I had to raise a lot of money for this thing. It was an exciting event. The critics — well, I don't remember it being the talk of the town. It always surprised me when I did these things, I loved them so much, and no one else would do something like that."

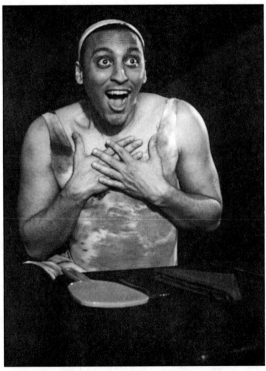

Aasif Mandvi developed his play, *Sakina's Restaurant* in classes with WH. (Photo by Martha Holmes.)

In another highlight from that time, Handman's student Aasif Mandvi created *Sakina's Restaurant*, another solo work, this one recreating the Village's East Sixth Street restaurant row, a locus of Indian immigrants to New York City. This is, of course, the actor who has become a staple of *The Daily Show with Jon Stewart*, the satirical faux-news program, as a "correspondent" reporting on various Third World and other affairs.

In the fall of 2012 Mandvi starred in Ayad Akhtar's *Disgraced*, a scorching drama presented at André Bishop's Lincoln Center Theater in the company's intimate new developmental space, the Claire Tow Theater atop the Vivian Beaumont. Strong reviews of the show, in which Mandvi played a lawyer living the very good life on Manhattan's Upper East Side whose rise up the corporate ladder is jeopardized when his Muslim identity in a post-9/11 world comes to the fore, led to several extensions. For months it was the most talked-about play in town and tickets at the tiny theater were impossible to come by. In April, 2013, *Disgraced* won the Pulitzer Prize for Drama.

It had been 14 years since *Sakina's Restaurant* won an Obie and kicked Mandvi's career into high gear. In October, 2012, we spoke in the Claire Tow's green room after a performance of *Disgraced.*

"Ayad sent me the script a couple of years ago," he told me. "It dealt with Muslim identity with a truthfulness I had never seen before. It had a lot to say about America now, and I knew it would be explosive. Naturally I told him I loved it and that I wanted to work with him on it — and of course that I wanted to star in it. So I've been involved in its development from early on.

"Frankly, I hadn't seen a script that spoke to me, to my experiences as a Muslim and as a brown person, so truthfully since, well, my own play," he continued. "And I credit Wynn for giving me the thread that links them. I was one of his acting students and I was developing one character, a guy who works in an Indian restaurant and has his own dreams and aspirations. Wynn focused right in on that and pushed me to create the whole universe in which he exists.

Aasif Mandvi backstage at Lincoln Center after a perfomance
of *Disgraced* (2013). (Photo by Jeremy Gerard.)

"And you know, that was the key," Mandvi continued.
"To Wynn, developing my experiences, *my* stories, was as
important — I think maybe even more important — than doing scene work from Shakespeare or Arthur Miller. Everyone
felt his ethic was about the dignity, the value of every person's
life. I think that's why so many of us solo artists came out
of the American Place, telling our stories to everyone who'll
listen. It's no accident. It's Wynn Handman, and it continues
to shape how I want to be an artist in the world."

'Why didn't I know, way back when?'

FROM THE BEGINNING, BACK in the Fifties, Handman juggled his lives in the theater, teaching students in his Carnegie Hall studio, producing important new work as artistic director of The American Place. In 1993, those two missions had fortuitously come together. As Oscar Hammerstein wrote in *The King and I*: *If you become a teacher / By your pupils you'll be taught.*

"I was not education minded," Handman said one morning in the winter of 2007, when we had gathered in his office with executive director David Kener and managing director Jennifer Barnette. "To me it was always second or third choice. I didn't want to hear about it. But the younger people on my staff did want to hear about it and talk about it and act on it. New programs popped up like Teachers Place, Urban Writes, Teamworks and a newly formed Education Committee. Chief educational activist was Elise Thoron, my cherished Artistic Associate."

At the same time, his acting students would come to class with novels and stories that provided them with characters to develop. Over the course of several months' work during the 1994-95 season, one such student, Tanya Little, had developed a monologue based on novelist Toni Morrison's *The Bluest Eye*. Little had even gone so far as to visit the Nobel laureate in her office at Princeton University, eager to secure her blessing for the nascent show.

"Toni Morrison said, 'If you want to do it for students, no box office, no publicity, just go ahead and do it. Don't tell me, just do it,' " Handman recalled. "As Tanya told me what Toni Morrison had said, I thought, *All right, we'll have a program called 'Literature to Life,' and we'll do it for students.* We started calling schools and began doing it in the seventy-five-seat Subplot theater during the week, and that's how Literature to Life was born."

"Even though it was exactly what you were doing from the beginning," Kener interjected.

But of course, playwrights, too, had always been essential to The American Place's artistic and social mission. "Why didn't I know, way back when I did Ed Bullins's plays and we had students to matinees who really got it, who said 'This is the first time I've ever seen my life on the stage'?" Handman wondered. "That should have signaled to me that there's something to this.

Billy Lyons in *The Things They Carried*, by Tim O'Brien, for the Literature to Life program. (Photo by Jennifer Barnette.)

142

"It really came into its own in 1982, when we first did *Do Lord, Remember Me*, the slave narratives. We booked Town Hall during Black History Month and had students coming to West Forty-third Street by the thousands."

Lou and Kelly Gonda, who had joined the small group of the company's most generous and loyal patrons, were so taken with the concept of Literature to Life that they personally underwrote, to the tune of $250,000, the creation of a Los Angeles arm of the program. As the program expanded, it became clear to both Kener and Barnette — and eventually to Handman as well — that the future of The American Place rested with this project and its young audiences. It was the perfect integration of Handman's classes and The American Place's commitment to developing new voices — and new audiences — for the theater.

"Just when I was thinking of Literature to Life as a new form of theater, Shakespeare intruded lines into my head," Handman recalled, "from the prologue of *Henry V* that perfectly describe my process and aim:

On your imaginary forces work
Think when we talk of horses, that you see them
Printing their proud hoofs i' the receiving earth;
For 'tis your thoughts that now must deck our kings,
Carry them here and there; jumping o'er times,
Turning the accomplishment of many years
Into an hour-glass

"I always had these sub-programs, whether the Women's Project, the American Humorists series, Literature to Life," Handman said. "David saw that Literature to Life could have a life of its own."

In fact, it was one that would prove to be a lifeline for The American Place. Time was running out at 111 W. 46th Street.

"WYNN HANDMAN DIDN'T KNOW WHAT HIT HIM."
Thus began a report in *New York* magazine on Septem-

ber 18, 2000. A few weeks earlier, Handman, contemplating the fact that his long term lease was going to run out in two years, began making inquiries about a renewal. That's when he learned for the first time that the theater was no longer his: A new landlord had arranged to turn it over to another nonprofit theater group, the Roundabout Theatre Company. He hadn't even been given an opportunity to put in a bid, although it's unlikely he would have been successful: The Roundabout is one of the largest theater companies in the country, with extremely deep pockets; indeed the new landlord was a member of the Roundabout's board.

More significantly, though, The American Place by 2000 had ceased functioning as a viable producing group. The last show to garner much audience interest was Jonathan Reynolds's savage satire, *Stonewall Jackson's House*, produced not on the main stage, but in the American Place's tiny basement space, was championed by several critics, notably Jack Kroll in *Newsweek* magazine.

"What matters about Wynn Handman that few people talk about is his courage," Reynolds says. "That's what matters about him. My plays don't fit into preconceived notions of what the nonprofit theater represents, which tends to be predictably lefty dogmatic. Although I gave The American Place Theatre a hit, what mattered to *me* is that years later, when I wrote *Stonewall Jackson's House* and took on several left-wing sacred cows, Wynn was the only one of the bunch who would produce it."

And by 2000, The American Place board was in no mood to fight for the lease. The last production of The American Place Theatre at 111 West Forty-sixth Street was *Living in the Wind*. The Roundabout refurbished and updated the space, which reopened as the beautiful Harold and Miriam Steinberg Center for Theatre, with the main stage dubbed the Laura Pels Theatre and, below it, a black box space for new works.

Nowhere in the Steinberg Center is there any mention of Wynn Handman or The American Place Theatre — not a plaque, cornerstone or any indication of the company and the leader responsible for bringing the space to life. They've been erased.

In 2003, the Literature to Life program took a major step forward with its presentation of the first Literature to Life Award to author Sue Monk Kidd, to inaugurate the presentation of *The Secret Life of Bees*. The publisher agreed to put the award on the cover of the paperback edition of the book, adding to the prestige.

The timing was no accident.

"That was a moment in the theater's history when it was go big, do something major, or say goodbye," Jennifer Barnette recalled. Penguin, the book's publisher, agreed to imprint the Literature to Life Award logo on paperback editions of the book.

"We were determined to get people to acknowledge the importance of this theater," said Kener.

One of the first Literature to Life presentations had been Handman's adaptation of Claude Brown's 1965 coming-of-age-in-America tale, *Manchild in the Promised Land.* "When I wrote this book, it was my life to literature," Brown remarked. "Now it's 'literature to life.' *Everything* comes full circle."

Nearly everyone who experienced Literature to Life became passionate about the program.

"Through a wisdom of the spirit that shapes each face-to-face meeting, there is a genius beyond compare. As director, Wynn Handman comprehends the significance of life at a different level. Through this art form he graciously shares truth with those in search of deeper meaning," wrote Don Nixon, director of The Centre for Performing and Visual Arts in Newnan, Georgia.

"Both young and old from every walk of life are changed for the better because of the mastery revealed through his works of art. The Literature to Life Program offers a provocative challenge to our town and through their dynamic force open doors, bridge gaps, cross hurdles and destroy walls that have shaped our existence in the past."

On May 21, 2007, some 500 people gathered at the historic Hudson Theater to honor Handman — to salute his 85th birthday and the 45th anniversary of the founding of The

American Place Theatre, which continues as the producer of the successful Literature to Life program.

The crowd included luminaries from all of Handman's lives: Eric Bogosian, former students like Chris Cooper; liberal politicians like former mayor David Dinkins, and countless people whose lives had been deeply affected by their association with The American Place.

What really was celebrated that night was an American character as original as Stieglitz, an iconoclast who has declined to cut his character to fit the model of the times, as Lillian Hellman might say.

"I can thank my lucky stars that I encountered a man like Wynn," an emotional Sam Shepard told the gathering that night, after telling some of the stories about decapitated chickens and one mighty arrogant young writer.

"More important than good nature is his unwavering support for new writing and its direct connection to the actor," Shepard continued. "When people ask me what I feel is missing from the theater these days, I have to say, it's passion. It's *not* economics. It's *not* politics. It's *not* a lack of ideas and influences. It's passion, pure and simple. And that's what people like Wynn generate just by their presence and their very character. I would like to thank him deeply for his generosity and belief in the power of new writing and in a theater of risk and adventure."

In October 2009, a one-man show called *County of Kings* opened at the Public Theater's *Under the Radar* festival.

"Most of the festival offerings are imported. This year, for the first time, the Public produced one of the shows. *County of Kings* — the title refers to the earlier name for the borough of Brooklyn — is a hip-hop-inflected coming-of-age tale written and performed by a young Hispanic poet named Lemon Andersen," I wrote in my review for Bloomberg News.

"Andersen conveys all this with irresistible feeling and sometimes powerful poetic images. It's impossible not to be drawn into this complex world expertly sketched out before an unchanging abstract backdrop. Director Elise Thoron's

Spartan staging adds immeasurably by cutting away almost everything but the language.

"*County of Kings* recalls the solo performances of John Leguizamo, and no wonder: The show was originated and is co-produced by The American Place Theatre, whose co-founder, Wynn Handman, first presented Leguizamo and has taught Andersen."

In *The New York Times,* Ben Brantley wrote, "*County of Kings* is in its outlines a conventional show-biz fable, not unlike the *Fame* movies, in which eager kids from hard-knock backgrounds 'learn how to fly' on the wings of talent. But Mr. Andersen invests the formula with a fine-grained grittiness of detail and a rapt love for words that is at least as strong as his love of hearing his own voice.

"The show's focus glides, like an old-fashioned biopic, down Manhattan, over the Hudson River and into a Brooklyn housing complex called the Courtyard. 'These are my streets, my stories,' says Mr. Andersen, admiring the retrospective view in wonder. 'How did I end up here?'"

How, indeed?

"Lemon came to my acting class, he was a hip hop poet," Wynn recalled. "I believe it was Bogosian or Leguizamo who pointed him to me. He was in class, where I did very basic work with him. He already was a charismatic performer — when he does his poems, *woo!* I had him do scenes from *Waiting for Lefty*, he was in my day class and he was really starting to catch on to acting. He expressed interest in being a teaching artist in the Literature to Life program. He saw *Manchild in the Promised Land,* and he said, 'Well, I can do that.' The American Place Theater was uniquely suited to him, to nurturing him. We paid him a stipend to write, to work, it took at least a year to develop that piece. He was coming here every day, assiduously, working it out."

"Lemon was doing it as a Literature to Life piece called *The Beautiful Struggle,*" Kener recalls. "It was going to be a book and that's what he came to The American Place Theatre for. We stayed with it, went to Portland with it. Mark Russell saw it here and said, 'Wynn, you've done it again.' He got it into the Public Theater's Under the Radar festival.

"Mr. Andersen has a distinctive talent that makes words sing in ways that insist you listen," Brantley concluded in his review. "But it's the drive that makes him glow. *Watch me*, he demands, in the first sentence of *County of Kings*. He guarantees that you do."

County of Kings was indeed an extraordinary theatrical event, the intersection of great writing, and a gifted acting talent. And it wasn't written by someone who knew he was a dramatist, which sort of makes it the quintessential American Place Theatre project. Had you seen *The Secret Life of Bees*, or *The Kite Runner* or any of the other works brought to immediate, urgent life in the program, you would come to realize that the remarkable thing about *County of Kings* is that is in very good company.

Literature to Life actress Cherita Armstrong in
Incidents in the Life of a Slave Girl. (Photo by Jennifer Barnette.)

The 2010 season of Literature to Life put 14 actors and 20 Master Teaching Artists to work in over 60 schools in New York City alone. Its shows play to upwards of 30,000 students annually in 175 performances a year. Literature to Life productions and residency workshops have been in over 100 communities across America since inception.

"What I think the key word is, is *waste,* " Handman says. "I could not stand the waste of talent in America in my field. Every day I see performances in my class that are wonderful. It's the same with writers."

Students' responses to the program show how deep the impact of one actor on a stage with a great story can go.

"I felt touched in my heart," student Ka Foon Lo wrote after seeing Gus Lee's *China Boy* performed by Wynn's student, Andrew Lee. "Your performance made me unable to control myself. Tears ran down my cheeks when you performed as Kai Ting's mother, who died abruptly from cancer…Your performance was spectacular. It was amazing to see a single actor take on all the different roles and characters in the play. Even though you performed on your own, I was able to understand each character's point of view and their intentions. You've done a great job."

Literature to Life has become the most sustained success in the history of The American Place Theatre, its long-running hit, its *A Chorus Line* — not the commercial-hit *A Chorus Line*, but an idea that carried the artistic integrity of an institution in its DNA while keeping its name and its mission before the theatergoing public and allowing The American Place to make a significant contribution to art and education.

For in Literature to Life, Handman found the best expression of the goal he first articulated nearly half a century ago: to restore the theater as a force against mediocrity and complacency. And in many ways, the battle is still just getting underway.

August, 2013

"What is most precious to you?"

IN MAY, 2013, WYNN HANDMAN celebrated his 91st birthday while continuing to teach his classes and finding new material for Literature to Life.

A year earlier, The American Place Theatre/Literature to Life merged with Young Audiences New York, an established nonprofit with six decades' experience as an advocate for, and presenter of, arts-related education and programming in the city.

"When faced with a seemingly insurmountable financial shortfall in Spring 2012, I insisted Wynn identify one thing," Jennifer Barnette told me, *"What is most precious to you?"*

"All ego was set aside, and he said that Literature to Life must continue reaching young people. That simple response allowed The American Place board and staff to make difficult decisions towards a single goal."

Both Kener and Barnette have moved on from The American Place Theatre and Literature to Life. But the merger has kept the program alive, along with the enduring name of its parent group, The American Place Theatre.

At this writing, Wynn and Bobbie Handman are taking their annual July vacation with the family in Nantucket. In the fall he will resume his acting classes near Carnegie Hall, turning out actors for the theaters and studios that have sprung up since first putting pencil to legal pad some fifty-two years ago.

"The Studio is as busy as ever," Wynn's amanuensis and teaching protégé Billy Lyons reported from the island. "We just re-signed the lease on the studio for another five years, believe it or not! Wynn's night and day classes are filled as usual, both with long waiting lists, and we've got about 50 prospective student auditions lined up in late August and September. I'm in my third year since Wynn endorsed me as a teacher at the studio. I uncovered the letter that Sandy Meisner wrote in 1951 recommending students to the class he was forming; he's doing the same to help me get started, using the same letter!

"With the merger, Young Audiences has made a firm commitment to stay strongly supportive of L2L and Wynn is intimately involved with the process. His daughter Laura has joined the Board of YANY and is hosting an event in Washington in September, presenting Wynn's adaptation of Jeanette Walls's *The Glass Castle*."

I asked Wynn whether he, in the tenth decade of life, felt ready to sum up. This was his reply:

"I don't look back with regret. There's nothing like Literature to Life anywhere else in the country. I'm as fulfilled now as I ever was. And I'm determined to make this decade of my life as fruitful and as exciting as the others."

A preliminary sketch by Kurt Lundell for the new theater
at 111 West 46th Street revealed that flexibility and intimacy
were of paramount importance.

Cutaway view of the new theater mainstage and audience.

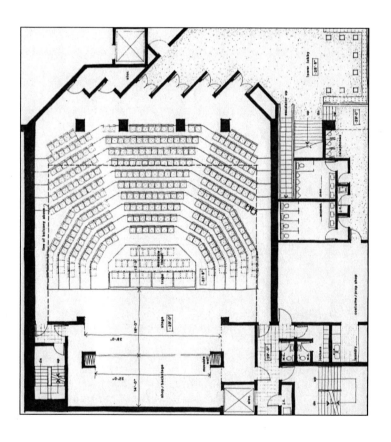

Seating and stage plan for the new theater.

APPENDIX B
PRODUCTION HISTORY
The American Place Theatre and Literature to Life

The American Place Theatre at St. Clement's Church

1964-1965

Robert Lowell	*The Old Glory: My Kinsman, Major Molineaux* and *Benito Cereno*
Ronald Ribman	*Harry, Noon And Night*
James Agee	*A Remembrance Of James Agee*

1965-66

William Alfred	*Hogan's Goat*
Paul Goodman	*Jonah*
Ronald Ribman	*The Journey Of The Fifth Horse*
May Swenson	*The Floor*
BruceJay Friedman	*23 Pat O'Brien Movies*
Robert Penn Warren	*Brother To Dragons*

1966-67

Ronald Milner	*Who's Got His Own*
Cecil Dawkins	*The Displaced Person*
Sam Shepard	*La Turista*
Niccolo Tucci	*Posterity For Sale*

1967-68

Frank Gagliano	*Father Uxbridge Wants To Marry*
Ronald Ribman	*The Ceremony Of Innocence*
Ed Bullins	*The Electronic Nigger And Others*
Robert Lowell	*The Old Glory: Endecott And The Red Cross*

1968-69

George Tabori	*The Cannibals*
David Trainer	*The Acquisition*
Phillip Hayes Dean	*This Bird Of Dawning*
Werner Liepolt	*The Young Master Dante*
Ronald Tavel	*Boy On A Straight Back Chair*
Kenneth Cameron	*Papp*

1969-70

Anne Sexton	*Mercy Street*
Charlie L. Russell	*Five On The Black Hand Side*
Charles Dizenzo	*The Last Straw*
David Scott Milton	*Duet For A Solo Voice*
Ed Bullins	*The Pig Pen*

1970-71

Joyce Carol Oates	*Sunday Dinner*
Steve Tesich	*The Carpenters*
George Tabori	*Pinkville*
Sam Shepard	*Back Bog Beast Bait and Cowboy Mouth*
Ira Gasman and Cary Hoffman	*What's A Nice Country Like You Doing In A State Like This?*
111 West 46th Street	

1971-72

| Ronald Ribman | *Fingernails Blue As Flowers* |

158

Steve Tesich	*Lake Of The Woods*
Jack Gelber	*Sleep*
Charles Dizenzo	*Metamorphosis*
Frank Chin	*The Chickencoop Chinaman*

1972-73

Robert Coover	*The Kid*
Phillip Hayes Dean	*Freeman*
Rochelle Owens	*The Karl Marx Play*
Steve Tesich	*Baba Goya*

1973-74

Frank Chin	*The Year Of The Dragon*
Ed Bullins	*House Party*
David Scott Milton	*Bread*

FESTIVAL OF SHORT PLAYS

Lonnie Carter	*Cream Cheese*
Robert Coover	*Love Scene*
Maria Irene Fornes	*Dr. Kheal*
William Hauptman	*Shearwater*

1974-75

S.J. Perelman	*The Beauty Part*
Straws In The Wind	*A Revue*
Sam Shepard	*Killer's Head And Action*
Jonathan Reynolds	*Rubbers* and *Yanks 3 Detroit 0 Top Of The Seventh*

AMERICAN HUMORISTS' SERIES

Jean Shepherd And The America Of George Ade
At Sea With Benchley, Kalmar And Ruby
Jean Shepard Plays Jean Shepard
We're In The Money- Humor And Songs Of The Depression

1975-76

Steve Tesich	*Gorky*
Phillip Hayes Dean	*Every Night When The Sun Goes Down*
Robert Lowell	*The Old Glory: Endecott* and *The Red Cross; My Kinsman, Major Molineaux* and *Benito Cereno*

AMERICAN HUMORISTS' SERIES

Conversations With Don B. - An Entertainment With Music Drawn From The Writing Of Donald Barthelme

1976-77

Jack Gelber	*Rehearsal*
William Hauptman	*Domino Courts And Comanche Café*
Jeff Wanshel	*Isadora Duncan Sleeps With The Russian Navy*
Ronald Ribman	*Cold Storage*

AMERICAN HUMORISTS' SERIES

Jules Feiffer's Hold Me!

1977-78

Elaine Jackson	*Cockfight*
Steve Tesich	*Passing Game*
Maria Irene Fornes	*Fefu and Her Friends*
Richard Nelson	*Conjuring An Event*

AMERICAN HUMORISTS' SERIES

Word Of Mouth—The Late Late Seventies Comedy Revue

1978-79

Annalita Marsili Alexander	*The Grinding Machine*
Steve Tesich	*Touching Bottom*

| Sam Shepard | *Seduced* |
| Jonathan Reynolds | *Tunnel Fever Or The Sheep Is Out* |

AMERICAN HUMORISTS' SERIES
AMERICAN HUMORISTS ON FILM

| Bruce Jay Friedman | *A Foot In The Door* |
| John Rothman (adaptation) | *The Impossible H.L. Mencken* |

THE WOMEN'S PROJECT

Patricia Bosworth, Caymichael Patten and Lily Lodge	*Choices*
Lavonne Mueller	*Warriors From a Long Childhood*
Joan Schenkar	*Signs of Life*
Rose Lehman Goldemberg	*Letters Home (Sylvia Plath)*

1979-1980

	Letters Home (Sylvia Plath)
Adaptation Michael Zettler	*Paris Lights The All Star Literary Genius Expatriate Revue*
Spalding Gray And Elizabeth Lecompte	*Rumstick Road*
Lavonne Mueller	*Killings On The Last Line*

AMERICAN HUMORISTS' SERIES

| Howard Teichmann | *Smart Aleck-Alexander Woollcott At 8:40* |
| William C. Osborne | *Sim: One Night With A Lady Undertaker From Texas* |

THE WOMEN'S PROJECT

| Sallie Bingham | *Milk of Paradise* |
| Gail Kriegel Mallin | *Holy Places* |

161

1980-81

John Rothman (Adaptation)	*The Impossible H.L. Mencken*
Richard Hamburger	*Memory Of Whiteness*
Emily Mann	*Still Life*
W.D. Snodgrass	*The Fuehrer Bunker*

AMERICAN HUMORISTS' SERIES

Sim One Night With A Lady Undertaker From Texas

Michael Zettler and Shelly Altman — *The Amazing Casey Stengel*

THE WOMEN'S PROJECT

Nadja Tesich	*After the Revolution*
Caroline Kava, Mel Marvin	*Constance and the Musician*
Emily Mann	*Still Life*

1981-82

Jane Stanton Hitchcock	*Grace*
Roscoe Lee Brown And Anthony Zerbe (Adaptation)	*Behind The Broken Words*
Bill Irwin	*The Regard Of Flight*

AMERICAN HUMORISTS' SERIES

Serious Bizness ("Laugh At Lunch")

A Crowd Of Two ("Laugh At Lunch")

THE WOMEN'S PROJECT

Paula Cizmar	*The Death of a Miner*
Kathleen Collins	*The Brothers*

1982-83

James De Jongh	*Do Lord Remember Me*
Ronald Ribman	*Buck*
	(co-production with Playwrights Horizon)
Donald Barthelme	*Great Days*

AMERICAN HUMORISTS' SERIES

Bruce D. Schwartz	*The Stage That Walks*
Michael Feingold (Adaptation)	*Speakeasy, An Evening Out With Dorothy Parker*

THE WOMEN'S PROJECT

Lavonne Mueller	*Little Victories*
Carol K. Mack	*Territorial Rites*
Terry Galloway	*Heart of a Dog*

1983-84

Various Authors	*The Vi-Ton-Ka Medicine Show*
James De Jongh	*Do Lord Remember Me*
Maria Irene Fornes	*The Danube*
Ted Talley	*Terra Nova*
	(co-production with Playwrights Horizon)

AMERICAN HUMORISTS' SERIES

Reinhard Lettau	*Breakfast Conversations In Miami*
Doug Skinner	*Pay Attention*

THE WOMEN'S PROJECT

Joan Micklin Silver and Julianne Boyd	*A....My Name is Alice*

1984-85

Ira Gasman & Cary Hoffman	*Whats A Nice Country Like You Still Doing In A State Like This?*
Stephen Wylie	*Rude Times*

AMERICAN HUMORISTS' SERIES

Ira Gasman And Cary Hoffman	*Whats A Nice Country Like You Still Doing In A State Like This?*
Conrad Pomerleau (Adaptation) ("Laugh At Lunch")	*Doings Of Gotham: The Wit And Humor Of Edgar Allan Poe*

JUBILEE! FESTIVAL

M.L.K. The Life And Times Of Martin Luther King
Celebration

Elizabeth Vandyke (Adaptation) Cabaret Series	*Love To All, Lorraine*

THE WOMEN'S PROJECT

Gina Wendkos and Donna Bond	*Four Corners*
Sallie Bingham	*Paducah*

1985-86

Jeff Wanshel Lyrics By Michael Feingold	*Times And Appetites Of Toulouse-Lautrec*
Eric Bogosian	*Drinking In America*
Vincent Smith	*Williams & Walker*

AMERICAN HUMORISTS' SERIES

Roy Blount Jr. ("Laugh at Lunch")	
John Martello (adaptation)	*Damon Runyon's Broadway*

THE WOMEN'S PROJECT

Lavonne Mueller	*Breaking The Prairie Wolf Code*

1986-87

Thomas Strelich	*Neon Psalms*
Cynthia Heimel	*A Girl's Guide To Chaos*

AMERICAN HUMORISTS' SERIES

John Valentine (adapation)	*James Thurber's Kintypes* ("Laugh At Lunch")

JUBILEE! FESTIVAL

Vinie Burrows (adaptation)	*Celebration: Her Talking Drum*

THE WOMEN'S PROJECT

Kat Smith	*Consequence*

1987-88

Alonzo D. Lamont, Jr.	*That Serious He-Man Ball*
Tony Lang	*Tallulah Tonight!*

AMERICAN HUMORISTS' SERIES

Roy Blount, Jr.	*Roy Blount's Happy Hour And A Half*
Various Authors	*Odd Jobbers*

JUBILEE! FESTIVAL

Shauneille Perry (adaptation)	*Celebration*
Lonnie Elder, III	*Splendid Mummer*

FIRST FLOOR THEATRE SERIES

Stephanie Silverman	*At The Back Of My Head*
Jane Gennaro	*The Boob Story*

THE WOMEN'S PROJECT

Suzanne Bennett and Liz Diamond	*The Snicker Factory: An Evening of Political Satire*

Maria Irene Fornes   *Abingdon Square*

1988-89

David Wolpe   *The Unguided Missile*
Clare Coss   *The Blessing*
Eduardo Machado   *The Burning Beach*

AMERICAN HUMORISTS' SERIES

Calvin Trillin's Uncle Sam
A. Whitney Brown's The Big Picture (In Words)

JUBILEE! FESTIVAL

Laurence Holder   *Zora Neale Hurston*

1989-90

Jeffrey Hatcher   *Neddy*
Laurence Holder   *Zora Neale Hurston*
Leslie Lee   *Ground People*

AMERICAN HUMORISTS' SERIES

Catherine Butterfield   *Bobo's Birthday*
Margery Cohen   *The Consuming Passions of Lydia E.*
(adaptation)   *Pinkham and Rev. Sylvester Graham*

1990-91

Joyce Carol Oates   *I Stand Before You Naked*
John Leguizamo   *Mambo Mouth*
Joseph Chaikin and   *The War In Heaven*
Sam Shepard
Joseph Chaikin And   *Struck Dumb*
Jean-Claude Van Itallie
Sam Shepard   *States Of Shock*
W.D. Snodgrass and   *Midnight Carnival and The Mask Man*
Faustwork Mask
Theatre

166

AMERICAN HUMORISTS' SERIES

Calvin Trillin's Words, No Music

1991-92

Theodora Skipitares	*The Radiant City*
Jane Gennaro	*Reality Ranch*
Roger Rosenblatt	*And*
Laurence Holder	*Zora Neale Hurston*

AMERICAN HUMORISTS' SERIES

Roger Rosenblatt   *Free Speech In America*

1992-1993

Thomas Strelich	*Dog Logic*
Matt Robinson	*The Confessions Of Stepin Fetchit*
Steven Wade	*On The Way Home*

1993-94

Kia Corthron	*Come Down Burning*
Barnaby Spring	*The Mayor Of Boys Town*

AMERICAN HUMORISTS' SERIES

Roger Rosenblatt   *Bibliomania*

Jimmy Tingle's Uncommon Sense

1994-95

Dael Orlandersmith	*Beauty's Daughter*
Norma Jean Darden	*Spoonbread and Strawberry Wine*
Wynn Handman (adaptation)	*Coming Through*

LITERATURE TO LIFE®

Toni Morrison	*The Bluest Eye*
Claude Brown	*Manchild In The Promised Land*

Ntozake Shange — *Sassafras, Cypress, and Indigo*
Sandra Cisneros — *The House On Mango Street*

1995-96

Norma Jean Darden — *Spoonbread and Strawberry Wine (Return Engagement)*
John Hockenberry — *Spoke Man*
Carson Kreitzer — *The Slow Drag*

LITERATURE TO LIFE®

Toni Morrison — *The Bluest Eye*
Claude Brown — *Manchild In The Promised Land*
Ntozake Shange — *Sassafras, Cypress, And Indigo*
Sandra Cisneros — *The House On Mango Street*
Amy Tan — *The Kitchen God's Wife*

1996-97

Jonathan Reynolds — *Stonewall Jackson's House*

LITERATURE TO LIFE®

Sandra Cisneros — *The House On Mango Street*
Amy Tan — *The Kitchen God's Wife*
Richard Wright — *Black Boy*

1997-98

Joseph Edward — *Fly*
Wynn Handman (adaptation) — *Coming Through (Encore, Queens Theatre In The Park)*
Tom Strelich — *Bafo (Best And Final Offer)*

LITERATURE TO LIFE®

Richard Wright — *Black Boy*
Cristina Garcia — *Dreaming In Cuban*

1998-99

Aasif Mandvi	*Sakina's Restaurant*
Laurence Holder	*Zora Neale Hurston: A Theatrical Biography (Return Engagement)*
Cristina Garcia	*Dreaming In Cuban: Rhythm, Rum Café Con Leche and Nuestros Abuelos!*
Michael John Garcés	*Agua Ardiente*
Julia Dahl	*Wonderland*

LITERATURE TO LIFE®

Richard Wright	*Black Boy*
Cristina Garcia	*Dreaming In Cuban*
Piri Thomas	*Down These Mean Streets* (Process Drama)
Tennessee Williams	*Glass Menagerie (Excerpts)*
Sarah Jones	*Surface Transit*
Aasif Mandvi	*Sakina's Restaurant* (Odyssey Theatre, Los Angeles, Ca.)
Claude Brown	*Manchild In The Promised Land*

LITERATURE TO LIFE®

Richard Wright	*Black Boy*
Cristina Garcia	*Dreaming In Cuban*
Piri Thomas	*Down These Mean Streets* (Process Drama)
Claude Brown	*Manchild In The Promised Land*
Wynn Handman (adaptation)	*Coming Through Ellis Island To JFK*

2000-2001

Michael Bradford	*Living In The Wind*
Lidia Ramirez	*I Love America*

LITERATURE TO LIFE®

Lidia Ramirez	*I Love America*

Wynn Handman (adaptation)	*Coming Through Ellis Island To JFK*
Claude Brown	*Manchild In The Promised Land*
Toni Morrison	*The Bluest Eye*
Richard Wright	*Black Boy*
James McBride	*The Color Of Water*
Sandra Cisneros	*The House On Mango Street*
Zora Neale Hurston	*Their Eyes Were Watching God* (Process Drama)

2001-2002

PUBLIC LIBRARY PERFORMANCE SERIES

Laurence Holder	*Zora*
Claude Brown	*Manchild In The Promised Land*
Wynn Handman (adaptation)	*Coming Through Ellis Island To JFK*

LITERATURE TO LIFE®

Lidia Ramirez	*I Love America*
Wynn Handman (adaptation)	*Coming Through Ellis Island To JFK*
Richard Wright	*Black Boy*
James McBride	*The Color Of Water*
Sandra Cisneros	*The House On Mango Street*
Laurence Holder	*Zora*
Zora Neale Hurston	*Their Eyes Were Watching God* (Process Drama)

2002-2003

LITERATURE TO LIFE®

Laurence Holder	*Zora*
Richard Wright	*Black Boy*
James McBride	*The Color Of Water*
Jamaica Kincaid	*Annie John*
Sandra Cisneros	*The House On Mango Street*

Gus Lee	*China Boy*
Claude Brown	*Manchild In The Promised Land*
James McBride	*The Color Of Water*

NATIONAL TOURS (WASHINGTON, DC)

Laurence Holder	*Zora*
Richard Wright	*Black Boy*
Claude Brown	*Manchild In The Promised Land*

2003-2004

LITERATURE TO LIFE®, NEW YORK

Laurence Holder	*Zora*
Richard Wright	*Black Boy*
Peter Ruocco (adaptation)	*Liberty Calling*
Sue Monk Kidd	*The Secret Life Of Bees*
Wynn Handman (adaptation)	*Growing Up A Slave*

NATIONAL TOURS (VARIOUS CITIES)

Laurence Holder	*Zora*
Richard Wright	*Black Boy*
Toni Morrison	*The Bluest Eye*

2004-2005

LITERATURE TO LIFE®, NEW YORK

Laurence Holder	*Zora*
Richard Wright	*Black Boy*
Wynn Handman (adaptation)	*Growing Up A Slave*
Claude Brown	*Manchild In The Promised Land*
Sue Monk Kidd	*The Secret Life Of Bees*
Cristina Garcia	*Dreaming In Cuban*

171

Tim O'Brien	*The Things They Carried*
Khaled Hosseini	*The Kite Runner*
Toni Morrison	*The Bluest Eye*
Wynn Handman (adaptation)	*Voices Of War*

NATIONAL TOURS (VARIOUS CITIES)

Sandra Cisneros	*The House On Mango Street*
Claude Brown	*Manchild In The Promised Land*
Wynn Handman (adaptation)	*Voices Of War*
Tim O'Brien	*The Things They Carried*
Toni Morrison	*The Bluest Eye*

2005-2006

LITERATURE TO LIFE®, NEW YORK AREA

Richard Wright	*Black Boy*
Cristina Garcia	*Dreaming In Cuban*
Jonathan Safran Foer	*Extremely Loud And Incredibly Close*
Wynn Handman (adaptation)	*Growing Up A Slave*
Khaled Hosseini	*The Kite Runner*
Claude Brown	*Manchild In The Promised Land*
Sue Monk Kidd	*The Secret Life Of Bees*
Tim O'Brien	*The Things They Carried*

NATIONAL TOURS (VARIOUS CITIES)

All above plus	
Sandra Cisneros	*The House On Mango Street*

2006-2007

LITERATURE TO LIFE®, NEW YORK AREA

Richard Wright	*Black Boy*

172

Jonathan Safran Foer	*Extremely Loud And Incredibly Close*
Jeannette Walls	*The Glass Castle*
Wynn Handman (adaptation)	*Growing Up A Slave*
Sandra Cisneros	*The House On Mango Street*
Harriet Jacobs	*Incidents In The Life Of A Slave Girl*
Khaled Hosseini	*The Kite Runner*
Claude Brown	*Manchild In The Promised Land*
Sue Monk Kidd	*The Secret Life Of Bees*
Tim O'Brien	*The Things They Carried*
Laurence Holder	*Zora*

NATIONAL TOURS (VARIOUS CITIES)

All above

2008-2009

LITERATURE TO LIFE®, NEW YORK CITY AND NATIONAL TOURS

Richard Wright	*Black Boy*
Jonathan Safran Foer	*Extremely Loud and Incredibly Close*
Jeannette Walls	*The Glass Castle*
Wynn Handman (adaptation)	*Growing Up a Slave*
Sandra Cisneros	*The House on Mango Street*
Harriet Jacobs	*Incidents in the Life of a Slave Girl*
Khaled Hosseini	*The Kite Runner*
Sue Monk Kidd	*The Secret Life of Bees*
Tim O'Brien	*The Things They Carried*
Laurence Holder	*Zora*
Frank McCourt	*Teacher Man*

2009-2010

LITERATURE TO LIFE®,
NEW YORK CITY AND NATIONAL TOURS

Richard Wright	*Black Boy*
Jeannette Walls	*The Glass Castle*
Wynn Handman (adaptation)	*Growing Up a Slave*
Sandra Cisneros	*The House on Mango Street*
Harriet Jacobs	*Incidents in the Life of a Slave Girl*
Khaled Hosseini	*The Kite Runner*
Sue Monk Kidd	*The Secret Life of Bees*
Tim O'Brien	*The Things They Carried*
Laurence Holder	*Zora*
Frank McCourt	*Teacher Man*
Lois Lowry	*The Giver*
Ray Bradbury	*Fahrenheit 451*

LIVING LIBRARY CLASSICS SERIES

(developed at The Flying E Ranch Artist's Residency sponosred by The Webb Center, Wickenburg, AZ)

As I Lay Dying	by William Faulkner
Invisible Man	by Ralph Ellison
Poems & Short Stories of Edgar Allan Poe	by Edgar Allan Poe
The Bluest Eye	by Toni Morrison
The Grapes of Wrath	by John Steinbeck
The Old Man and the Sea	by Earnest Hemingway
The Poetry of Emily Dickinson	by Emily Dickinson
Their Eyes Were Watching God	by Zora Neale Hurston
To Kill A Mocking-bird	by Harper Lee

174

2010-2011

**LITERATURE TO LIFE®,
NEW YORK CITY AND NATIONAL TOURS**

Richard Wright	*Black Boy*
Jeannette Walls	*The Glass Castle*
Wynn Handman (adaptation)	*Growing Up a Slave*
Sandra Cisneros	*The House on Mango Street*
Harriet Jacobs	*Incidents in the Life of a Slave Girl*
Khaled Hosseini	*The Kite Runner*
Sue Monk Kidd	*The Secret Life of Bees*
Tim O'Brien	*The Things They Carried*
Laurence Holder	*Zora*
Frank McCourt	*Teacher Man*
Lois Lowry	*The Giver*
Ray Bradbury	*Fahrenheit 451*
Greg Mortenson	*The Three Cups of Tea*

LIVING LIBRARY CLASSICS SERIES

(developed at The Flying E Ranch Artist's Residency sponosred by The Webb Center, Wickenburg, AZ)

As I Lay Dying	by William Faulkner
Invisible Man	by Ralph Ellison
Poems & Short Stories of Edgar Allan Poe	by Edgar Allan Poe
The Bluest Eye	by Toni Morrison
The Grapes of Wrath	by John Steinbeck
The Old Man and the Sea	by Earnest Hemingway
The Poetry of Emily Dickinson	by Emily Dickinson
Their Eyes Were Watching God	by Zora Neale Hurston

To Kill A Mocking-bird	by Harper Lee

2012-2013   (Merger with Young Audiences NY)
**LITERATURE TO LIFE®,
NEW YORK CITY AND NATIONAL TOURS**

Richard Wright	*Black Boy*
Jeannette Walls	*The Glass Castle*
Wynn Handman (adaptation)	*Growing Up a Slave*
Sandra Cisneros	*The House on Mango Street*
Harriet Jacobs	*Incidents in the Life of a Slave Girl*
Khaled Hosseini	*The Kite Runner*
Sue Monk Kidd	*The Secret Life of Bees*
Tim O'Brien	*The Things They Carried*
Laurence Holder	*Zora*
Frank McCourt	*Teacher Man*
Lois Lowry	*The Giver*
Ray Bradbury	*Fahrenheit 451*
Piri Thomas	*Down These Mean Streets*
Junot Diaz	*The Brief Wondrous Life of Oscar Wao*

LIVING LIBRARY CLASSICS SERIES
(developed at The Flying E Ranch Artist's Residency sponosred by The Webb Center, Wickenburg, AZ)

As I Lay Dying	by William Faulkner
Invisible Man	by Ralph Ellison
Poems & Short Stories of Edgar Allan Poe	by Edgar Allan Poe
The Bluest Eye	by Toni Morrison
The Grapes of Wrath	by John Steinbeck

The Old Man and the Sea	by Earnest Hemingway
The Poetry of Emily Dickinson	by Emily Dickinson
Their Eyes Were Watching God	by Zora Neale Hurston
To Kill A Mockingbird	by Harper Lee

2013-2014   (Young Audiences New York)

**LITERATURE TO LIFE®,
NEW YORK CITY AND NATIONAL TOURS**

Richard Wright	*Black Boy*
Jeannette Walls	*The Glass Castle*
Wynn Handman (adaptation)	*Growing Up a Slave*
Sandra Cisneros	*The House on Mango Street*
Harriet Jacobs	*Incidents in the Life of a Slave Girl*
Khaled Hosseini	*The Kite Runner*
Sue Monk Kidd	*The Secret Life of Bees*
Tim O'Brien	*The Things They Carried*
Laurence Holder	*Zora*
Frank McCourt	*Teacher Man*
Lois Lowry	*The Giver*
Ray Bradbury	*Fahrenheit 451*
Piri Thomas	*Down These Mean Streets*
Junot Diaz	*The Brief Wondrous Life of Oscar Wao*
Lemon Anderson	*County of Kings*

LIVING LIBRARY CLASSICS SERIES

(developed at The Flying E Ranch Artist's Residency sponosred by The Webb Center, Wickenburg, AZ)

As I Lay Dying	by William Faulkner
Invisible Man	by Ralph Ellison

Poems & Short Stories of Edgar Allan Poe	by Edgar Allan Poe
The Bluest Eye	by Toni Morrison
The Grapes of Wrath	by John Steinbeck
The Old Man and the Sea	by Earnest Hemingway
The Poetry of Emily Dickinson	by Emily Dickinson
Their Eyes Were Watching God	by Zora Neale Hurston
To Kill A Mocking-bird	by Harper Lee

Awards & Honors

VILLAGE VOICE *OBIE* AWARDS

1982: "For uncompromising commitment to unconventional and daring plays," a special citation and grant for $5,000.

1999: Sustained Achievement: Wynn Handman

  Special Citation: Aasif Mandvi, *Sakina's Restaurant* and:

1965: Best American Play: *The Old Glory*,
  Costume designer: Willa Kim, *The Old Glory*

1966: Best American Play: Ronald Ribman, *Journey of the Fifth Horse*

1967: Distinguished Play: Sam Shepard, *La Turista*

1968: Distinguished Design: Robert LaVigne, *Endicott and the Red Cross*

1969: Best Play: Ron Tavel, *Boy On a Straight Back Chair*

1976: Distinguished Performance: Tony Lo Bianco, *Yanks 3, Detroit 0, Top of the Seventh*

1977: Playwriting: Maria Irene Fornes, *Fefu and Her Friends*

Playwriting: William Hauptman, *Domino Courts*

Distinguished Performance: Marian Seldes, *Isadora Duncan Sleeps With the Russian Navy*

1981: Best Production: Emily Mann, *Still Life*

Performance: John Spencer, *Still Life*

Performance: Mary McDonnell, *Still Life*

Performance: Timothy Near, *Still Life*

1986: Playwriting: Eric Bogosian, *Drinking in America*

1991: Distinguished Performance: John Leguizamo, *Mambo Mouth*

OTHER AWARDS AND HONORS TO WYNN HANDMAN:

1993: Lucille Lortel: Off-Broadway Lifetime Achievement Award Wynn Handman;

1994: Rosetta LeNoire Award in 1994 from Actor's Equity Association: Wynn Handman, in recognition of his artistic achievements and contribution to the "universality of the human experience in American theatre"

1990, 1998: Audelco Award for Excellence in Black Theatre: Wynn Handman for directing *Zora Neale Hurston* and *Fly*

1996: Carnegie Mellon Drama Commitment to Playwriting Award Wynn Handman;

Working Theatre's Sanford Meisner Service Award for "leadership in disseminating the arts to working people,"

The New Federal Theatre honor in 2001.

City College of New York Townsend Harris Medal, "in recognition of his distinguished contributions to his chosen field of work and the welfare of his fellow men."

Doctor of Humane Letters, University of Miami, 2003

SOME OF WYNN HANDMAN'S STUDENTS

Alec Baldwin	Carol Lawrence
Connie Britton	John Leguizamo
Red Buttons	Susan Lucci
James Caan	Aasif Mandvi
Kathleen Chalfant	Phyllis Newman
Chris Cooper	Dennis Quaid
Brad Davis	Kim Raver
Michael Douglas	Burt Reynolds
Sandy Duncan	Tony Roberts
Mia Farrow	Mercedes Ruehl
Richard Gere	Debra Jo Rupp
Lauren Graham	Anna Deavere Smith
Joel Grey	Mira Sorvino
Allison Janney	Christopher Walken
Raul Julia	Denzel Washington
Frank Langella	Joanne Woodward

C

E

G

Grace, 162

Graduate, The,

Graham, Lauren, 181

Graham, Martha, 76

Grapes of Wrath, The, 174, 175, 176, 177, 178

Gray, Spaulding, 8, 118, 161

Great Days, 163

Green, Adolph, 105, 106

Greenland, Narsassuak, 18

Greenwich Village, 12, 28, 46, 63, 64, 101, 116, 133

Grey, Joel, 14, 23, 51, 52, 181

Grinding Machine, The, 160

Ground People, 166

Growing Up A Slave, 171, 172, 173, 174, 175, 176, 177

Group Theatre, 21, 45

Gussow, Mel, 127

Guthrie Theatre, 97

Guthrie, Sir Tyrone, 28

Guys and Dolls, 54

Gypsy, 74

H

Hagen, Uta, 7

Hair, 12, 97, 105

Hadassah, 86

Hall, Adrian, 28

Hamburger, Richard, 162

Hamlet, 28

Hammarskjöld, Dag, 31

Hammerstein, Oscar, 141

Kazan, Elia, 35, 36, 56

Keating, John, 44

Keaton, Diane, 102

Keats, 50

Keitel, Harvey, 74

Kener, David, 141, 142, 143, 145, 147, 148, 151

Kennedy, Jackie, 54

Kennedy, John F., 32, 40

Kennedy, Robert F., 68

Kern, Jerome, 45

Kerr, Walter, 52, 54, 61, 63, 83, 98, 110, 113, 120, 121, 124, 127, 128

Kid, The, 159

Kidd, Sue Monk, 145, 171, 172, 173, 174, 175, 176, 177

Killens, John O., 70,

Killer's Head, 96, 106, 107, 130

Killings On The Last Line, 161

Kim, Randy, 96, 97, 98, 99

Kim, Willa, 179

King and I, The, 141

King Jr., Martin Luther, 68

King Jr., Woodie, 15, 60, 61, 62, 68, 70, 86

King, Carole, 123

Kincaid, Jamaica, 170

Kitchen God's Wife, The, 168

Kite Runner, The, 148, 172, 173, 174, 175, 176, 177

Kornfield, Lawrence, 27, 55

Koshel, Terry, 39

Kramer Vs. Kramer, 11

Kreitzer, Carson, 168

N

O

Q

R

U

X

Y

ACKNOWLEDGEMENTS

In the spring of 2006, Wynn Handman asked me to write a history of The American Place Theatre. I agreed to take on the project with the understanding that I would be able to tell the complete story, though obviously I would be coming to it from the vantage point of friendship with the Handmans and a record of critical support for shows at The American Place.

Self-evidently, then, this is not a scholarly account, nor is it meant to be. My goal has been to write an oral history, defined by Wynn's voice, with contributions from many of the major figures in his theater's extraordinary history. The quotation that begins the book is from *Antoine and the Théâtre-Libre*, a similar work written a century ago by my granduncle.

Everyone quoted in this book was interviewed by me, in person or by telephone, and I thank all of them for their time, patience and stories. Any errors in the telling, however, are mine alone.

Wynn Place Show would not have been possible without the support of The American Place Theatre Board of Trustees. Nor would it have ever gotten off the ground, let alone come to completion, without the urging, help, assistance, prodding and guidance of former executive director David Kener and former managing director Jennifer Barnette. Kurt Kelly and Denise Wilbanks offered invaluable indexing and fact-checking help.

Wynn's teaching protege Billy Lyons brought unwavering devotion and enthusiasm to every detail of the manuscript while helping to sort through Wynn's files and memories.

The late Martha Holmes captured the life of The American Place Theatre with a photographer's eye for detail and an artist's insight into the creative process. I thank her daughters, especially Terry Koshel, for joining me in this project.

John Leguizamo's enthusiasm for writing the foreword was typical of the feelings expressed by Wynn's students and collaborators.

An early version of the first chapter was published in *American Theatre* magazine.

Laura Handman played a critical role in bringing the elements of this book together for publication. Liza Handman contributed her expertise and many hours to preparing the photographs and illustrations.

Kathleen McAchren and Nancy A. Zoubek of Jones Day were tireless in working out the legal details for the manuscript.

At Smith and Kraus, I want to especially thank Marisa Smith, Elizabeth Monteleone and Larry Harbison for creating a beautiful book.

My wife, Carla Wittes, patiently combed the manuscript; her suggestions were invaluable.

Bobbie and Wynn: Barbara Handman died in the early morning of November 14, 2013. No one championed this book more fervidly than she, and Wynn read every word of it to her over its many drafts. She was my silent editor and advocate, for which I'm so grateful. As for Wynn: He opened his heart, his voluminous files and his prodigious memory to me across innumerable hours of interviews, his recollections miraculously sharpening with each revisit. He is magnificent. I'd thank him, but, well, I've written this book for him.

WH and Bobbie, surrounded by family, in an undated photograph.
(Photo courtesy Wynn Handman.)

Jeremy Gerard has written about the lively arts since 1975, most recently as the chief drama critic for Bloomberg News. He was the Broadway reporter for *The New York Times*, chief drama critic for the *Dallas Morning News* and *Variety*, and columnist and reviewer for *Soho Weekly News* and *New York* magazine. He has taught criticism and cultural reporting in the graduate school of journalism at Columbia University. A member and past president of the New York Drama Critics Circle, Gerard has served as a juror for the Pulitzer Prize for Drama, including as jury chairman, and been a guest judge for the Village Voice Obie Awards and the Lucille Lortel Awards. His book *Act Two: Creating Partnerships and Setting Agendas for the Future of the American Theater*, about the Second American Congress of Theater, was published in 2003 by Theater Communications Group. A Distinguished Alumnus of Purchase College, Gerard lives in New York City.